CANTERBURY COUSINS

The Eucharist in Contemporary Anglican Theology

OWEN F. CUMMINGS

Paulist Press
New York/Mahwah, NJ

Cover and book design by Lynn Else

Library of Congress Cataloging-in-Publication Data

Cummings, Owen F.
    Canterbury cousins : the Eucharist in contemporary Anglican theology / Owen F. Cummings.
        p.   cm.
    ISBN-13: 978-0-8091-4490-7 (alk. paper)
    1. Lord's Supper—Anglican Communion. 2. Anglican Communion—Doctrines. I. Title.
BX5149.C5C86 2007
234'.163088283—dc22

                                                        2007029394

Published by Paulist Press
997 Macarthur Boulevard
Mahwah, New Jersey 07430

www.paulistpress.com

Printed and bound in the
United States of America

CONTENTS

Amico in Domino,

M. Francis Mannion

PREFACE

This is a book by a Roman Catholic, written primarily but not only for Roman Catholics. In the almost forty years since the end of the Second Vatican Council (1962–65), the Catholic Church has developed in a variety of different ways. A greater appreciation of Holy Scripture has emerged through the lectionary for Mass, through the widespread appropriation of modern approaches to biblical studies, and through numerous scripture-study groups and programs. Liturgy is now in the vernacular language, and all the sacramental rites of the church have been revised. The Missal of Pope Paul VI has been a great success. It could be argued that two of the major achievements of Vatican II have had to do with word and Eucharist, Christ feeding us with his word and with himself.

The area of ecclesiology has been another growth point in the history of the church since the council. This is especially the case with ecumenism. If *Lumen gentium*, the conciliar Constitution on the Church, speaks of the nature and structure of the church, and *Gaudium et spes* of the church's witness to and service of the world, *Unitatis redintegratio*, the Decree on Ecumenism, invites Catholic engagement with other Christian traditions in the cause of Christian unity. We have moved some way since Pope Pius XI's encyclical letter, *Mortalium animos* (1928), which forbade Roman Catholics from participating in such ecumenical initiatives as the Faith and Order Movement. The council's Decree on Ecumenism persuasively encourages Catholics to be involved in ecumenism, and church documents since then continue this encouragement.

Two related passions, flowing out of Vatican II, drive this book: the Eucharist and an ecumenical concern for the church. If the Eucharist makes the church, if the body of Christ makes the body of Christ, then Eucharist and the unity of the church must go

v

hand in hand. If the church's unity is wounded, the Eucharist must be part of the medicine of healing. This is not a plea for instantaneous intercommunion, but a recognition of the indissoluble link between Eucharist and church. Part of the difficulty for Catholics especially is a real lack of knowledge, of genuine awareness, of how other Christians perceive and practice Eucharist. This book attempts to remedy the deficit in respect to the Anglican Communion, especially the Church of England. It attends to a number of twentieth-century theologians who have written about the Eucharist, some better known than others, but all contributing to a rich tapestry of eucharistic meaning. Some limited attention is also given to key church documents that deal with or are pertinent to eucharistic theology and appreciation. The aim is not so much to be comprehensive as selective, a selectivity directed by and to Catholic appreciation and discovery. Those informed about contemporary Anglican theology will notice no mention of John Macquarrie, who has developed a comprehensive eucharistic theology. The omission is entirely deliberate due to the fact that I have already written on Macquarrie's eucharistic theology in my *John Macquarrie: A Master of Theology* (New York and Mahwah, NJ: Paulist Press, 2001), and the interested reader is referred to that publication.

As Catholics move through the book, my immediate hope is that they will come to recognize members of the Anglican Communion as cousins, "Canterbury Cousins." My ultimate hope, of course, is that this gradual recognition will one day, through God's grace, flourish into dining at the same eucharistic table.

Chapter 1

Introducing
Canterbury and Rome

At the opening of the Holy Year door at St. Paul-Outside-the-Walls in Rome on January 18, 2000, Pope John Paul II was accompanied by the representative of the ecumenical patriarch of Constantinople and by Archbishop George Carey of Canterbury. Apparently, the Holy Year door would not yield to Pope John Paul until he was assisted in the enterprise by the representative of the ecumenical patriarch and Archbishop Carey. The joint and cooperative touch of all three ecumenical leaders opened the door![1] The church leaders, praying for unity together, sought to heal the East-West wounding of the church in the eleventh century and the sixteenth-century fragmentation of the Western Church. The church, wounded in its unity, is wounded in its mission.

The See of Rome dates back to the first-century Roman Christian community and its preeminence to the martyrdom of Saints Peter and Paul. The See of Canterbury began in 597 with the arrival of St. Augustine, who established his first church in that city. Augustine had been directed by the See of Rome in the person of Pope Gregory the Great to organize the church in England into provinces, with archbishops at York and London. From the outset, the place of London was taken by Canterbury, which has been the see of the archbishop of the southern province of England, the Primate of All England. In the sixteenth century the church in England became separated from the wider Catholic Church with its center in Rome. Canterbury and Rome entered into a period of estrangement that was to last for more than four hundred years. This period of estrangement came to an end with Vatican II's Decree on Ecumenism, promulgated on November 21, 1964, and the catalyst for much ecumenical exchange between Rome and Canterbury.

1

Theological dialogue has taken place on a range of important issues, for example, the Eucharist, ordination, authority, salvation. However, some problematic initiatives, and problematic not only from the point of view of Rome—such as the ordination of women to the presbyterate and the episcopate, as well as various moral and ethical issues—may have given the unfortunate impression that ecumenical relations between Rome and the Anglican Communion are not of great importance anymore. This is far from the case. Representative Catholic and Anglican bishops, thirteen pairs of each, under the leadership of Cardinal Edward Cassidy of the Pontifical Council for the Promotion of Christian Unity and Archbishop George Carey, archbishop of Canterbury, met at Mississauga near Toronto May 14–20, 2000, to discuss ecumenical matters. Recognizing real difficulties, but spending at least two hours each day in prayer and liturgy, the bishops came to recognize that over the ecumenical decades since Vatican II Anglicans and Catholics had drawn closer to the goal of full and visible communion than anyone would have dreamed possible. Such a forthright recognition from the episcopal leadership of both communions is a beacon of great ecumenical hope, and yet one still has the impression of a very considerable ecumenical impasse between Canterbury and Rome.

Perhaps one of the root difficulties is the sheer lack of accurate information and awareness at the popular level in the two communions, including the level of clergy awareness. This is particularly the case in respect to the Eucharist. From a Catholic perspective, often one will hear Catholics affirm that Anglicans do not believe in the eucharistic presence of Christ, and it comes as a shock to them to realize that this is not the case. Again there remain among Catholics some very crude and ill-informed presuppositions about the Anglican Communion's distinctive emergence in the sixteenth century at the time of King Henry VIII. However, the changes that brought about the Anglican Church of the sixteenth century are far from straightforward. While it would be utterly misleading to reduce such a complex phenomenon as the English Reformation to a simplistic outline, it is nevertheless helpful from the perspective of this book on some twentieth-century Anglican approaches to the Eucharist to treat of it under the following headings: the church in England on the eve of the Reformation; from Henry VIII to

Elizabeth I; the Book of Common Prayer, 1559; ecumenical rapport between Rome and Canterbury after Vatican II.

On the Eve of the Reformation

Advocating a certain caution in interpreting the Reformation period, the Anglican bishop-theologian, Stephen Sykes, has written:

> Attitudes towards the writings and activities of the leading reformers, continental as well as British, have a way of being predetermined by attitudes towards the Reformation itself, with passages and episodes being deployed merely as illustrations.[2]

Bishop Sykes's point is well taken. Rather than adopting some a priori position to the events of the sixteenth century, a more informed historical approach will attend to the actual data from the period, such as they are. It is frequently assumed by historians of the period that the church in England, on the eve of the Reformation, was a church in need of a thoroughgoing reform, a church with which the majority of the English faithful were singularly dissatisfied. This seems not to have been entirely the case. More recent investigations offer an alternative reading of the situation, especially the contribution of church historian Eamon Duffy. At the beginning of his book, *The Stripping of the Altars*, Duffy sets out his thesis and then spends the rest of the book verifying this thesis in detail:

> Late mediaeval Catholicism exerted an enormously strong, diverse and vigorous hold over the imaginations and the loyalty of the people up to the very moment of the Reformation. Traditional religion had about it no particular marks of exhaustion or decay, and indeed in a whole host of ways, from the multiplication of vernacular religious books to adaptations within the national and regional cult of the saints, was showing itself well able to meet new needs and new conditions.[3]

The ordinary people were basically satisfied and content with their inherited form of Catholic Christianity. Investigation of wills from the time shows a large number of people willing property and money to the church, and, while this in itself does not establish an absolute satisfaction with the religious and theological environment—indeed, how would that ever be possible!—it surely is an acknowledgment of their affection and devotion. Consequently, some historians argue that the Reformation never won the wholehearted allegiance of the majority of the English people. The very term *Reformation* is probably so ingrained in our sociocultural and religious discourse that it would be very problematic not to use it, but it is not altogether satisfactory. The term *Reformation* might suggest that "a bad form of Christianity was being replaced by a good one."[4] This is where the revisionist work, based on close analysis of the actual data by some contemporary historians, is changing perceptions of the Reformation period in England.

This is not to deny that the new reformed theology from the European Continent was not making headway in English academic and ecclesiastical circles. It certainly was, and especially in the University of Cambridge. Nor is it to deny that there were problems in the church that needed attention. The church is always in need of reform—it is a hospital for sinners—but to speak of *the* Reformation may both deflect attention from the continuous need to reform, repent, and configure our lives to Christ and also suggest that the reform of the sixteenth century itself sits free of such constants.[5]

From Henry VIII to Elizabeth I

There can be little doubt that the Reformation in England was inextricably knit into the constitutional problem of King Henry VIII (r. 1509–47) having no male heir to his throne. Henry's desire to divorce his wife, Catherine of Aragon, the wife of his dead brother Arthur whom he had married with papal dispensation, had reached a canonical impasse with Rome. Henry then sought his desired annulment of the marriage from the English clergy, and in 1534, in the Act of Supremacy, proclaimed himself the supreme head of the church in England. Between 1535 and 1540 Henry suppressed all the monasteries and convents, distributing their lands and properties to his nobles. The paradox is that, while these events were taking place, Henry himself was not especially receptive to the ideas of the continental reformers. In point of fact, in 1521 Pope Leo X conferred on Henry the title *Defensor Fidei*, "Defender of the Faith," for a treatise he had written against Martin Luther entitled *The Defense of the Seven Sacraments*. Probably not too much should be made either of Henry's theological competence or of this title, which Henry valued more for its political statement. It gave status similar to that of the honorific titles of the emperor and the king of France, "Most Catholic" and "Most Christian." The church of which Henry had declared himself the head was really a form of Catholicism without the pope. However, the spread of Lutheran ideas was enabled in England especially through a number of clerical figures associated with the University of Cambridge from at least 1520. Henry may not have favored such Protestant ideas personally, but he was aware of their power not only in terms of doctrinal revision but also politically. At his death in 1547 Henry, though personally committed to Catholic doctrine and practice, was particularly conscious of these incipient Protestant influences in England. This would account for the facts that he refused any substantive liturgical change during his reign, but also left his young son (Edward VI), still a minor, in the hands of Protestant noblemen. He was looking to the old church and to the new church, as it were. In that basic sense Henry anticipated in some degree the Elizabethan religious settlement that was yet to come, a settlement that sat between Catholicism on the one hand and Protestantism on the other, and sat somewhat uncomfortably and uneasily.

With the accession of King Edward VI, the archbishop of Canterbury, Thomas Cranmer, moved speedily to produce his first edition of the Book of Common Prayer in 1549, containing an outline of the Mass in English and communion under both kinds.[6] Cranmer, one of the chief architects of the reform in England, has left his stamp firmly on the liturgy right up to the present day, and was a truly fascinating character in his own right. A theologian at Jesus College, Cambridge, Cranmer was very receptive to the renewed emphasis on the study of Holy Scripture emerging from humanist and reformist thinkers. Yet, at the same time, the Cambridge Cranmer was not a thoroughgoing reformer. Indeed, in the comments in his own hand in the margin of Cranmer's personal copy of Bishop John Fisher's *Confutation of the Lutheran Assertion*, Cranmer is often in agreement with the unmistakably Catholic Fisher. He is probably best thought of as standing in the conciliarist tradition. It is not always adequately recalled that the reform-minded but conciliarist Council of Constance (1414–18) was but one hundred years before the Reformation. Cranmer was concerned over Luther's attitude to the councils of the church. He was deeply attached to the principle and practice of church councils, so much so that one contemporary church historian concludes:

> Perhaps one might see this reverence for the authority of the General Council as the golden thread which runs through Cranmer's theological progress: the one constant to which he always returned, even when in later years his appeal for a General Council was addressed to Wittenberg, Zurich and Geneva rather than to Rome.[7]

Nonetheless, it must be said that Cranmer's second edition of the Book of Common Prayer in 1552 was to go much further in the promotion of Protestant ideas so that the eucharistic liturgy is really very different from the medieval Mass. If one tries to relate the clear eucharistic differences between the first and second editions of the Book of Common Prayer, the best way forward is probably to regard the first edition as preparatory for the more radical revision represented by the second.

Some examples from the revised eucharistic liturgy will establish the point. Traditionally, at the reception of holy communion, the communicant was met with words about the eucharistic gifts preserving body and soul unto everlasting life. That was changed in 1552 to:

> Take and eat this in remembrance that Christ died for thee, and feed on him in thy heart by faith, with thanks-

6

giving.... Drink this in remembrance that Christ's blood was shed for thee, and be thankful.[8]

This is a radical departure from traditional eucharistic understanding, avoiding any language that smacked of transubstantiation. Should there be any doubt, a sentence in the rubrics for the communion service reads as follows: "And if any of the bread or wine remain, the Curate shall have it to his own use." Diarmaid MacCulloch comments:

> Bread and wine there had been at the beginning of the service, and bread and wine there had been at the end of it. Once they had served their purpose, and treated with the reverence which the solemnity of the service demanded, they could be taken home to the parsonage and used as the human creations which they were.[9]

Despite his evident revisionist eucharistic theology, Cranmer's 1552 service did not please those who were further to his left in terms of their reformist tendencies. Within months King Edward VI died and was succeeded by Mary Tudor, who was a devout Catholic. Often Mary's attempt to restore Catholicism is understood only in purely reactionary terms, but there is abundant evidence to show that the Marian authorities' program was "not one of reaction but of creative reconstruction," absorbing what they interpreted as positive during the reigns of Henry VIII and Edward VI.[10] Thus, the revived interest in preaching was retained by the Marian authorities; the possession of Bibles and Bible reading by the people were never condemned. At the same time, there was a distinct push to regain the power of sacrament, typical of Catholicism, alongside word, typical of the reform. The Marian restoration sent a series of reform-minded theologians into exile on the continent of Europe, and there liturgical revision continued to be discussed and debated. Some advocated more or less the eucharistic celebration of Cranmer's 1552 book—the Prayer Book party—and their basic theological position was ultimately to prevail, while the more radical such as John Knox argued for a ritually and theologically slimmer Eucharist, virtually a simple commemorative meal.

Mary's attempt at restoration was not to last very long. In November 1558 after her death, Elizabeth came to the throne and immediately set about the rehabilitation of Henry VIII's reforms, still not unfairly described as Catholicism without the papacy. She was not to have an entirely free hand at liturgical revision along more or less Henrician lines, perhaps with the restoration of the 1549 prayer book. As the exiles returned home, so did their debates about the prayer book, and most especially the Eucharist. They would not be content with a pre-Edwardian liturgical settlement. Eventually in 1559 Elizabeth restored the prayer book of 1552 with a few alterations, alterations that were all in a conservative mold but, even so, "no one really wanted the Prayer Book they had been given."[11] It satisfied neither the more Catholic wing of the church nor the more Puritan-reformed wing of the church. This 1559 Book of Common Prayer remained in constant use until 1604, when some very minor changes were made. Again, some further changes were made with the 1661/62 revision when the monarchy was restored to England after the Puritan commonwealth period. These latter changes were of no great substance, so that the Elizabethan book of 1559, based on the 1552 book, has remained in place in Anglican worship until the prayer book revisions of the late twentieth century, and so it is to this book we must go for the dominant Anglican sense of the Eucharist.

The Book of Common Prayer, 1559

"The Order for the Administration of the Lord's Supper, or Holy Communion" in the 1559 Book of Common Prayer begins with the priest's recitation of this beautiful collect:

> Almighty God, unto whom all hearts be open, all desires known, and from whom no secrets are hid: Cleanse the thoughts of our hearts by the inspiration of thy Holy Spirit, that we may perfectly love thee, and worthily magnify thy holy name; through Christ our Lord. Amen.

There follows a penitential service in which the priest rehearses the Ten Commandments and the people ask for God's mercy. The collect of the day is now prayed and the sequence of the epistle, the gospel, the creed, and the sermon falls into place. Exhortation culled from an anthology of New Testament texts is given to the people and then the collection is taken up "and put into the poor men's box."

Clergy and people then pray for the whole of the church: for the universal church, for Christian rulers and especially Queen Elizabeth, for the bishops and clergy, for all the people of the church and particularly this congregation. If the curate "shall see the people negligent to come to the Holy Communion," he exhorts them "as [they] love [their] own salvation, that [they] will be partakers of this Holy Communion." The priest addresses those about to receive Holy Communion:

> Draw near, and take this holy Sacrament to your comfort; make your humble confession to Almighty God before this congregation here gathered together in his holy name, meekly kneeling upon your knees.

Having made an acknowledgment and confession of sin, the priest offers to all present "the comfortable words" of Christ:

> Come unto me all that travail and be heavy laden and I shall refresh you. So God loved the world, that he gave his only begotten Son, to the end that all that believe in him should not perish but have life everlasting.

The eucharistic prayer begins with the usual words: "Lift up your hearts," and after the preface the priest kneels down "at God's board" and prays the eucharistic prayer. Immediately prior to the eucharistic prayer is a very striking prayer that combines both Reformation and Catholic emphases:

> We do not presume to come to this thy table (O merciful Lord) trusting in our own righteousness, but in thy manifold and great mercies. We be not worthy so much as to gather the crumbs under thy table, but thou art the

same Lord, whose property is always to have mercy. Grant us therefore (gracious Lord) so to eat the flesh of thy dear Son Jesus Christ, and to drink his blood, that our sinful bodies may be made clean by his body, and our souls washed through his most precious blood, and that we may evermore dwell in him, and he in us. Amen.

If the reference to trusting in God's righteousness reflects a constant of Reformation theology, there can be no doubt that the realism of the eucharistic language in the rest of the prayer is profoundly and traditionally Catholic. The Anglican systematic theologian, John Macquarrie, says of the words "to eat the flesh of thy dear Son Jesus Christ and to drink his blood" that they are "so vividly realistic that we must pause to ask just what it is that we eat and drink in the Lord's Supper."[12] This vivid realism upon which Macquarrie comments is nothing other than the eucharistic realism that had been traditional from the patristic through the medieval church, and indeed is to be found in Martin Luther himself, who defended the eucharistic presence of Christ against Huldrych Zwingli at the Marburg Colloquy in 1529. In the eucharistic prayer the Eucharist is acknowledged as "the perpetual memory" of the unique sacrifice of Christ on the cross. We may see here the Lutheran and general Reformation dislike for the notion of sacrifice attached to the Eucharist, but the language of the Eucharist as a *memorial* of Christ's sacrifice on the cross is not foreign to Catholic theology, nor indeed to the decrees of the Council of Trent. Prior to the words of institution, God is besought that "we...may be partakers of his most blessed Body and Blood...." Once again, *partakers* seems to suggest eucharistic realism in the Catholic sense. After the ministers have received communion, the people kneel to receive. This is especially significant because in the prayer book of 1552 there was a rubric, known as the "Black Rubric," the entire tone of which suggested that the posture of kneeling had nothing to do with adoring the eucharistic Christ. This "Black Rubric" is absent from the 1559 book. At communion the minister says to the communicants:

> The body of our Lord Jesus Christ which was given for
> thee, preserve thy body and soul into everlasting life: and
> take and eat this, in remembrance that Christ died for
> thee, and feed on him in thy heart by faith, with thanks-
> giving.

After presenting the bread the minister offers the cup with the
words:

> The blood of our Lord Jesus Christ which was shed for
> thee, preserve thy body and soul into everlasting life: and
> drink this in remembrance that Christ's blood was shed
> for thee, and be thankful.

These two utterances present first Catholic eucharistic realism, but
then qualify that with "feeding on Christ by faith," a typical
Reformation sentiment. When communion is over, the Lord's
Prayer is recited, the Gloria is sung, and the final blessing is given.

Even this cursory examination of the 1559 liturgy establishes
that the language of the Elizabethan liturgy is beautiful. Such a
liturgy, however, could not appeal *tout court* to the tradition of
Catholicism. Nor could it speak to the desires of the more
Protestant-Puritan elements of the church. It reflects in many
respects a compromised eucharistic theology, and has been a source
of controversy among Anglicans ever since.

To say that the Elizabethan prayer book of 1559 represents a
compromised theology, however, is not an exhaustive statement.
The Book of Common Prayer has nourished and sustained the
eucharistic faith of countless Anglicans over the centuries. People
have lived saintly lives on its theology and spirituality. Eucharistic
faith and theology do not remain frozen in a timeless fashion, but
develop in relation to a host of factors. One of the factors that has
assisted and promoted liturgical renewal and the development of
eucharistic reflection in the Anglican Communion has been the
ecumenical rapprochement between Canterbury and Rome that
has taken place since Vatican II.

Canterbury and Rome after Vatican II

The Decree on Ecumenism of the Second Vatican Council was promulgated on November 21, 1964. It represents the formal advent of the Catholic Church into the ecumenical movement of the twentieth century. Chapter three of the decree takes up the question of "Churches and Ecclesial Communities Separated from the Roman Apostolic See." Of the Anglican Communion the decree says: "Among those in which some Catholic traditions and institutions continue to exist, the Anglican Communion occupies a special place."[13] Though it does not say it in so many words, we may reasonably infer that the decree is alluding to the Catholic elements of theology and liturgical practice, among other things, that have remained in place since the Elizabethan Settlement. Concerning the Eucharist, paragraph 22 of the decree is of special importance:

> The ecclesial communities separated from us lack that fullness of unity with us which should flow from baptism, and that especially because of the lack of the sacrament of orders they have not preserved the genuine and total reality of the Eucharistic mystery. Nevertheless, when they commemorate the Lord's death and resurrection in the Holy Supper, they profess that it signifies life in communion with Christ and they await his coming in glory.[14]

The paragraph states that from a Catholic point of view "the genuine and total reality of the eucharistic mystery" has not been preserved in the separated churches and ecclesial communities of the West. It is noteworthy that it does not in an a priori fashion disallow eucharistic reality in these churches. It maintains that the eucharistic mystery "in its genuine and total reality" has not been preserved. That statement opened the door to dialogue about the Eucharist. The decree went on to say, "Dialogue should be undertaken concerning the true meaning of the Lord's Supper, the other sacraments, and the Church's worship and ministry."[15]

"The Joint Declaration on Cooperation" of Pope Paul VI and Archbishop Michael Ramsey formally opened the dialogue between Rome and Canterbury on March 22, 1966. The church historian, Owen Chadwick, gives us a fine glimpse of Pope Paul VI's openness to and appreciation of Anglicanism, quite remarkable for the time:

> Paul had more knowledge of English religion than any of his predecessors...he had a respect, unusual in Italian prelates of those days, for the English religious tradition. "I have great affection for your Book of Common Prayer," he said to a visiting English layman, Sir Gilbert Inglefield, who told him about the Series 2 experimental liturgy in England, "you must not abandon it. It is very beautiful poetry." He was a friend of George Bell, the Bishop of Chichester, who helped him towards an understanding of Anglicanism.[16]

Paul's openness was echoed in the receptivity of Archbishop Michael Ramsey, a passionate supporter of the ecumenical cause. This "Joint Declaration" inaugurated between the two communions a serious theological dialogue that, founded on the gospels and on the ancient common traditions, has produced a number of important agreed statements, and later we shall attend in some detail to the agreed statement on the Eucharist, "The Windsor Statement."

As well as the ecumenical dialogue, Anglican theologians have continued to reflect and write about the Eucharist in ways that enrich the entire Christian tradition, and in the chapters ahead we shall recognize some of the more important contributions. My hope and prayer is that those who look to Canterbury as the center of their Christian communion, and celebrate and reflect upon the Eucharist in the tradition of Canterbury will be seen by Catholics as cousins, and cousins to whom in God's grace we are drawing closer.

Notes

1. Alex J. Brunett, "Harvesting the Past, Planting for the Future: Our Pilgrimage Together," *Ecumenical Trends* 30 (2001): 1.

2. Stephen Sykes, *Unashamed Anglicanism* (Nashville: Abingdon Press, 1995), 33.

3. Eamon Duffy, *The Stripping of the Altars* (New Haven and London: Yale University Press, 1992), 4.

4. John Bossy, *Christianity in the West 1400–1700* (Oxford: Oxford University Press, 1985), 91.

5. See Christopher M. Bellitto, *Renewing Christianity: A History of Church Reform from Day One to Vatican II* (New York and Mahwah, NJ: Paulist Press, 2001) for a fine study of church reform and renewal throughout the entire Christian tradition.

6. For a comprehensive grasp of the Edwardian religious scene, see Diarmaid MacCulloch, *The Boy King Edward VI and the Protestant Reformation* (Berkeley and Los Angeles: University of California Press, 1999).

7. Diarmaid MacCulloch, *Thomas Cranmer* (New Haven and London: Yale University Press, 1966), 29.

8. Cited from MacCulloch, *Thomas Cranmer*, 506.

9. MacCulloch, *Thomas Cranmer*, 79.

10. Duffy, *The Stripping of the Altars*, 526.

11. Geoffrey J. Cuming, *A History of Anglican Liturgy*, 2nd ed. (London: Macmillan, 1982), 98.

12. John Macquarrie, *A Guide to the Sacraments* (New York: The Continuum Publishing Company, 1997), 119.

13. Walter M. Abbott and Joseph Gallagher, eds., *The Documents of Vatican II* (New York: The America Press, 1966), 356.

14. Ibid., 364.

15. Ibid.

16. Owen Chadwick, *Michael Ramsey: A Life* (Oxford: Clarendon Press, 1990), 317.

Chapter 2

CHARLES GORE

In 1901, the very beginning of the twentieth century, Charles Gore published *The Body of Christ*.[1] Charles Gore (1853–1932) was arguably the most important Anglican theologian at the beginning of the twentieth century, and one of the greatest of all Anglican thinkers and teachers. His religious upbringing was Low Church, reflecting the Reformation rather than the Catholic aspect of the now four-hundred-year-old Elizabethan religious compromise, but apparently at the age of eight or nine he had an experience that changed his ecclesial direction. He read a book, *Father Clement*, by a Protestant author in which a Catholic priest is converted to Protestantism. This is how Gore's biographer describes it:

> When the boy read in this book a description of confession and absolution, fasting, the Real Presence, the use of incense, and similar matters, he felt instinctively and at once an attraction for this sort of sacramental religion. It was "the religion for me."[2]

This book, it would seem, took Gore over to the Anglo-Catholic side.

After ordination Gore was made vice-principal of Cuddesdon, the Anglican seminary outside Oxford, and then the first principal of Pusey House. One of his colleagues there was Frank Edward Brightman, the liturgiologist. It is inconceivable that Brightman did not share his passion for and knowledge of matters liturgical with Gore. His awareness of and reference to different rites and liturgies in *The Body of Christ* undoubtedly owe something to Brightman. He taught in the university, gave spiritual counsel and direction, and was much sought after.

Gore continued his own studies in theology, especially in the Latin and Greek fathers. They nourished his own spiritual life as much as his growing ecclesiology. Gore was at the center of the controversial book, *Lux Mundi*, which came out in 1889. Its objective was to put the Catholic faith into right relation with modern intellectual and moral issues. As a result of it, when he was appointed bishop of Worcester in 1901, some regarded him as a radical, while others saw him as leaning toward Rome. Later, he became bishop of Birmingham, and then in 1911 was translated to Oxford. Resigning in 1919, Gore lived in London and continued to write theology, giving, for example, the prestigious Gifford Lectures, published as *The Philosophy of the Good Life*.

The Body of Christ

As noted, *The Body of Christ* came out in 1901. The bishop of London, Mandell Creighton, had summoned a roundtable conference in 1900 with the purpose of thinking through the different emphases in eucharistic theology in the Church of England. There was little agreement, but this conference forms the backdrop to Gore's book, the response to which is well put by G. L. Prestige: "The book was vigorously attacked from the Protestant side, enthusiastically welcomed by men of the Tractarian tradition."[3] Tractarians were the Catholic wing of the church, following in the tradition of the Oxford movement of the nineteenth century.

Gore's principle and methodology lay in "purging" or "enlarging" the current tradition through recourse to the fonts of the tradition, most especially the scriptures and the fathers of the church. He believed that the ancient church held the doctrine of a real presence without transubstantiation, and it is to this ancient eucharistic doctrine that the Church of England appealed. His desire was to set out the Anglican teaching on the Eucharist against this background, and so to avoid what he took to be the extremism on both sides of his church, Protestant and Anglo-Catholic.

Some Sacramental Presuppositions

Gore held that the fundamental idea of sacrifice lies in communion between the deity and his worshipers, a communion brought about "by joint participation in the living flesh and blood of a sacred victim."[4] For Christians this generic view of sacrifice is made specific in taking, eating, and drinking the eucharistic gifts; through the consequent fellowship/communion in the glorified manhood of Christ, we become partakers in his divinity. This is the common teaching of the first Christian millennium and the climax of the Christian religion:

> This—the propagation of Christ's manhood by the transmission of his Spirit, or Christ *in us* the hope of glory—is truly the culminating point of our religion.... It was felt to be so at least through all the first twelve centuries of our era.[5]

It is this notion of appropriating Christ's glorified manhood through the Eucharist and so participating in his divinity that is the first and basic presupposition for the doctrine of the Eucharist.

The second presupposition is an adequate understanding of sacrament, an understanding that recognizes that "a spiritual gift should be communicated by God to man through the medium of a material ceremony."[6] Gore believed that there was a tendency in Protestantism so to separate the spiritual and the material that the latter was rejected as unworthy of God. He, on the other hand, was at pains to show that the spiritual in us feeds upon material symbols. Thus, for example, a handshake is the sacrament of friendship, a kiss the sacrament of love. Both are material, empirical realities, and yet the reality of the handshake or kiss transcends, but does not and cannot eliminate, the material element. This is key not only to Gore's eucharistic thinking, but to his profound grasp of the incarnation. The incarnation is the coming together of the Divine Logos in human nature. In the incarnation the spiritual—the Divine Logos—is not possible without the material—human nature. In that way the Eucharist may be understood as the extension of the incarnation.

Nonetheless, these spiritual events, embodied in material reality, may be recognized only with the eyes of faith.

A third presupposition is the sociality of the sacraments. The sacraments are social rites through and through, "the divine provision against spiritual individualism."[7] They are social rites not only in the sense that the gathered Christian assembly celebrates them, but also in their social and moral consequences, what might be called the realization of Christian brotherhood, another theme very dear to Gore's heart.

The flesh and blood of Christ received in the Eucharist must be "the 'flesh' and 'blood' of the glorified Christ, for no other exists."[8] Though the same Christ, by the same Spirit, is ministered to us through the other sacraments, it is in holy communion that we have the most complete participation in Christ's glorified humanity. Though not teased out in detail, Gore had a sense of the manifold presence of Christ in the entire celebration of the Eucharist. Christ is present throughout the whole celebration. "What [the consecration] brought about was not the presence of Christ—he was already there—but his adoption of the Church's gifts to become his body and his blood."[9]

Eucharistic Presence

It is essential to know what Gore meant by *spiritual* in reference to the sacraments. *Spiritual* means God-as-Spirit at work in humanity. This divine working requires material mediation, for we are material beings destined for "spiritual" completion in God. Against any form of Gnosticism, ancient or modern, a sacrament is God-as-Spirit giving himself to us, operating through created, material reality.

The eucharistic words of the consecration effect a new reality:

> The words of our Lord, "This is my body: this is my blood"…must be taken to mean that the elements in the eucharist become by the operation of the Holy Ghost something mysterious and holy that they were not before, but without ceasing to be in all material respects exactly what they already were.[10]

To regard the eucharistic elements as other than material while recognizing the transformation that they have undergone spiritually is, for Gore, a eucharistic Monophysitism, the tendency to annihilate and absorb the human in the divine. This Monophysite tendency becomes for him transubstantiation. For Gore the doctrine of transubstantiation is corrupt because, in abolishing the material elements of bread and wine, it overthrew the nature of a sacrament, in which material objects and events embody and manifest the action of God. If transubstantiation happened in Christology, it would abolish the incarnation. There would be no human element. It would be a form of Monophysitism. In another essay Gore wrote, "Transubstantiation in eucharistic doctrine is the analogue of nihilianism with regard to the incarnation."[11] John Macquarrie is careful to point out that Gore may have fastened on to the corrupt form of transubstantiation, rather than the form given to it by Aquinas, for example. For Gore transubstantiation became successful in the Berengarian controversy, and is found in the crude oath that Berengar had to take about the presence of Christ. Transubstantiation, thus understood, became an unacceptable metaphysical intrusion into Christian doctrine. For all such reasons, maintains Gore, the Anglican Communion should continue to hold to the ancient doctrine of Christ's presence, but without the unnecessary medieval metaphysical accretion of transubstantiation.

Gore advocates what he calls the spiritual presence of Christ in the eucharistic gifts, where spiritual expresses "not what is unreal, but what is profoundly real."[12] That is spiritual in which the Holy Spirit effectively manifests itself and effectively controls. Such is the case par excellence with the eucharistic gifts. The purpose of this spiritual but real presence is to be received in holy communion by persons who share this faith, not individualistically but as the faith of the church as a whole.

For this reason, that Christ is present to be *received*, Gore is opposed to eucharistic reservation. Eucharistic reservation as a permanent presence of Christ seems opposed, to him, to "the indwelling of Christ in the members of his body, of which it is the glory of the sacrament to be the earthly instrument."[13] Devotion to the reserved sacrament does not help Christians to realize the universal presence of God in creation, or the indwelling of Christ in themselves as church.

This position did not please all in the Anglo-Catholic wing of the church, even those who were otherwise appreciative of Gore's contribution. For example, Eric Mascall, whom we shall discuss in a subsequent chapter, believes this aspect of Gore's eucharistic theology to be thoroughly unsatisfactory. Mascall was an advocate of eucharistic devotions centered on the reserved sacrament, and insofar as he finds Gore's understanding of the eucharistic presence disallowing such devotions, he finds it defective. Mascall as an avowed Thomist also takes issue with Gore's description of transubstantiation as an intrusion into church doctrine. While he feels that scholastic metaphysics is intrusive, Mascall points out that Gore goes on to appeal to his own philosophy, what Mascall describes as "a quasi-Kantian idealism," to elucidate his understanding of eucharistic presence.[14] Whether one subscribes to the substance-based metaphysics of Aquinas and Mascall or not, one may still ask if Gore has grasped transubstantiation accurately. It is arguable that Gore's stated predilection for the eucharistic theologies of the patristic era, extensively quoted throughout *The Body of Christ*, makes the further metaphysical refinement of Christ's presence in the scholastic era unnecessary. Remaining content with the *thatness* of Christ's eucharistic presence, without probing philosophically the *howness* of that presence, seems to be Gore's position. The vagueness of this view, however, raises as many questions as it hopes to solve, and remains finally unpersuasive. While one accepts that the presence of Christ is sheerly mysterious, there is an ineluctably interrogative aspect to us that requires some degree of satisfaction.

Eucharist as Sacrifice

Gore recognized that the church has affirmed that the Eucharist is sacrificial from the earliest days.[15] A sacrifice is the acknowledgment of God as the source of all blessings and the desire to be held in holy communion with him. The Eucharist is this in the finest way.

The Eucharist is the Christian sacrifice, because what is there made present to faith in the midst of the worshipping Church is the body and blood of Jesus, as our perpetual and all-sufficient sacrifice.[16]

It does not bring about any ongoing surrender of Christ to death, but is the real commemoration of that unique sacrificial death.[17] Any notion of Christ being resacrificed is abhorrent to Christian faith, and detracts from that unique self-gift on Calvary. He believes that the notion of Christ's being resacrificed is present in the Roman Catholic tradition, whether they are "popular misconceptions" or "theological errors."[18]

The end or purpose of Christ's offering himself for us is to bring humanity back into union with God and with one another. "What he does first for us, he must ultimately do in us."[19] Communion in and with God is the essential end of sacrifice. This ever-evident principle has the fathers of the church

perpetually reiterating that we become his body by sharing his body: that by eating his flesh we pass into his flesh.... The sacrifice is the sacrifice of the whole body, and the communion is the communion of the whole body.[20]

All our human sacrifices are caught up in this one, unique sacrifice of Christ, head and members, and we enter by grace into his redemptive achievement. All our human sacrifices are coextensive with the entire life of the church, caught up in the eucharistic representation of Christ's unique sacrifice.

Conclusion

Toward the end of *The Body of Christ* Gore posits the need to restore the Eucharist to its central place in Christian life, especially on the Lord's Day. "With nothing short of this may we be content."[21] But he recognized equally that it must be a celebration in which the communion of the people takes place, and not which they simply attend. And he further recognized that this holy communion must extend out beyond the confines of the liturgical celebration to confirm again and again the communion of all in Christ. "By receiving his body from above, we are to become his body on earth."[22] Eucharistic Christians, eschewing a "miserable individualism," act eucharistically

> in those habitual and considerate good works of love by which the body of Christ on earth is bound together. It is by mutual kindness and sociability, real and equal consideration, large forbearance and tolerance of differences of disposition and taste and opinion; by a vivid belief that if one member suffer all the members suffer with it; and by true regard for the whole interests of each other, in body as well as spirit, in respect of outward conditions as well as those that are inward.[23]

Writing in 1953, Eric Mascall considered that despite the "intrinsic excellence" of Gore's *The Body of Christ*, it "has fallen into undeserved neglect."[24] Perhaps Roman Catholics in discovering Gore's eucharistic theology, its strengths and weaknesses from a Roman Catholic point of view, may in some way promote an Anglican rediscovery of Gore that may aid and abet the ecumenical cause.

Notes

1. Charles Gore, *The Body of Christ* (London: John Murray, 1901).

2. G. L. Prestige, *The Life of Charles Gore* (London and Toronto: William Heinemann, 1935), 4.

3. Ibid., 220–21.

4. Gore, *The Body of Christ*, 13.

5. Ibid., 31.

6. Ibid., 36.

7. Ibid., 42.

8. Ibid., 66.

9. Ibid., 105.

10. Ibid., 111.

11. Charles Gore, *Dissertations on Subjects Connected with the Incarnation* (London: John Murray, 1895), 283, cited in John Macquarrie, *A Guide to the Sacraments* (New York: The Continuum Publishing Company, 1997), 130.

12. Gore, *The Body of Christ* 124.

13. Ibid., 138–39.

14. Eric L. Mascall, *Corpus Christi* (London–New York–Toronto: Longmans Green, 1953), 152–55.

15. Gore, *The Body of Christ* 157.

16. Ibid., 267.

17. Ibid., 174–75.

18. Ibid., 181.

19. Ibid., 199–200.

20. Ibid., 204–13.

21. Ibid., 276.

22. Ibid., 286.

23. Ibid., 287.

24. Mascall, *Corpus Christi*, 138.

Chapter 3

WILL SPENS AND OLIVER CHASE QUICK

Will Spens

"Six feet tall, wearing rimless pince-nez, with a highly domed head, a slow tread, a tight-lipped expression, and little small-talk, Spens was a formidable personality." This is how Sir William (Will) Spens (1882–1962) is described in *The Dictionary of National Biography*.[1] Very few theologians outside the Church of England will have come across Will Spens, and perhaps few enough within that church itself. He was one of the most influential laymen in the Church of England in the first half of the twentieth century. In 1915 he published *Belief and Practice*, and from 1922 to 1938 he was a member of the Archbishops' Commission on Doctrine. He wrote a significant essay on the Eucharist in 1926 that remains worth reading both for its catholicity and its incisiveness, an essay that displays theological insight and something of his religious devotion.

Sacraments and Symbols

Spens's declared intention is to provide an understanding of the Eucharist out of the tradition, but in ways that will communicate its centrality to people today. Symbols come into play when words are found to be sheerly inadequate. The Christian sacraments are symbols, but they are effectual symbols, not merely conveying a message, but bringing about a result.[2] The sacraments bring about an effectual result because they are determined by God himself, "invested by divine authority with certain spiritual or supernatural elements." The sacraments do not eliminate the natural properties

24

of the signs, but so "supersede [them] that we can rightly speak of the objects as wholly changed and transfigured." For Spens, then, symbol is no "mere" symbol. Symbol has its own rightful ontology, and the sacraments an ontology divinely determined. This important point will be returned to when we come to describe his understanding of the eucharistic presence of Christ, but first we turn to the doctrine of eucharistic sacrifice.

The Eucharistic Sacrifice

Spens believes that a stranger present at the Eucharist would naturally describe it as a sacrificial rite, and he enters the discussion through the lens of social anthropology.

> If a student of comparative religion, not otherwise acquainted with Christianity, were to enter a church where the Holy Mysteries were being celebrated, and were afterwards asked what kind of service he had been attending, he would undoubtedly say that it was some sacrificial rite; and he would find his answer endorsed if he were to turn from the service which he had witnessed to the earliest narratives of its institution.[3]

A very clear, if perhaps phenomenological position on eucharistic sacrifice. Spens, however, does not leave it at that. He proceeds to draw attention to the obviously sacrificial dimensions of meaning in the New Testament narratives so that he is able to connect closely the Last Supper with the Calvary sacrifice of Christ.[4] The actual words of Christ in the gospel accounts, "Take, eat, this is my body; take, drink, this is my blood," spoken on the occasion of the Last Supper can only mean that the apostles were thereby made partakers in the sacrifice in which he was to be the victim. This, for Spens, is the obvious meaning of the Lord's words.

Turning to St. Paul in 1 Corinthians 11, Spens finds the same emphasis on eucharistic sacrifice. Though his fleeting reference to the mystery religions shows him to reflect the "History of Religions" attitude of New Testament studies of his time, that in no wise detracts from the sacrificial aspect to which he wishes to draw attention:

> St. Paul's language seems definitely to require this view; for he was writing for persons familiar in a greater or lesser degree with Mystery Religions, and it is incredible that he should not have guarded his language far more carefully, had he not regarded the Eucharist as a sacrifice, and believed that devout ritual participation in this sacrifice secured and conditioned participation in spiritual blessings.[5]

Chapter 6 of St. John's Gospel is similar in understanding, even if the language in which that understanding is expressed differs somewhat. As to the reformed interpretation of John 6, that our Lord was not talking about eating his body, and therefore, entering into his sacrificial action, but rather was talking about being receptive to his teaching, Spens dismisses this:

> If by eating his flesh our Lord is taken to have meant merely the reception of his teaching, then his language as recorded could only be pronounced unaccountably misleading and provocative.[6]

The realism of the dominical eucharistic words, especially in this concern with sacrifice, cannot be gainsaid, except through the most unreal hermeneutical subtleties. If there has been Anglican resistance to this notion of eucharistic sacrifice, it is for Spens understandable. There is, he maintains, in the dominant Catholic understanding the suggestion of an immolation of Christ in every celebration of the Mass. For Spens this notion is both repellent and unnecessary.

The Eucharistic Presence

"The doctrine of the Real Presence, more perhaps than any other element in eucharistic teaching, is charged with all the warmth of Christian devotion."[7] Spens speaks of it as a "special presence," an idea with which Christianity cannot dispense. No less than ancient Israel with its awareness of God's omnipresence, yet also its acknowledgment of his special presence in the Shekinah, Christianity too balances its general sense of God's gracious, enveloping presence with a "special presence." The bread and wine are changed in the celebration of the Eucharist. They are changed "by consecration."

> Regard being had to their sacrificial context, this is the natural meaning of the description of the consecrated elements, in relation to their consumption, as our Lord's body and blood—his body given for us and his blood shed for us.[8]

In line with his understanding of effectual symbol noted above, the bread and wine *become* the body and blood of Christ through their becoming effectual symbols. He does not use language of substance to speak of this reality. He prefers the more dynamic term *transvaluation*. If anything, his language comes close to the contemporary view of transignification, as in this sentence:

> In and through consecration those complexes of opportunities of experience which we call bread and wine are changed, not by any change in the original opportunities of experience, but by the addition of new opportunities of experience which are equally ultimate and have far greater significance.[9]

If one is concerned about the ontology of the eucharistic change because of language like *opportunities of experience*, language that seems very subjective, there is no need for concern. The change is indeed real. The use of such words as *new, equally ultimate*, and *far greater* outweighs any suspicion attendant upon *significance*. Should that not allay concern and anxiety about the orthodoxy of expression, consider this very unambiguous passage:

> The identity between our Lord's glorified body and his natural body must be held to consist in the facts that

opportunities of experience which each includes, and normally conditions, are directly determined by that nature which our Lord assumed at his Incarnation; and that in each case the whole complex of opportunities of experience exists as such in immediate dependence on that nature and affords immediately an expression of it. All this is, however, also the case in regard to the eucharistic body or blood.[10]

Though he appears not to advocate the more traditional term *transubstantiation*, the eucharistic conversion may be translated into different philosophical expressions, maintains Spens. Further underscoring his Catholic conviction of the ontological eucharistic change, Spens is in favor of eucharistic adoration, but he does not develop it in this essay. Spens was an almost exact contemporary of Oliver Quick, and so it is to Quick that we now turn our attention.

Oliver Chase Quick

Oliver Chase Quick (1885–1944) was the son of an Anglican priest, born at Sedbergh vicarage, Yorkshire. After studies at Oxford he was ordained a priest in 1912. He had pastoral experience in a number of places, served in World War I, taught theology at the University of Durham, and became Regius Professor of Divinity at Oxford in 1939. According to his biographer, Leonard Hodgson, Quick was dissatisfied with "facile restatements of Christian dogma."[11] His first published article was entitled "The Value of Mysticism," reflecting the renewed interest in that subject as a result of the work of Friedrich von Hügel and Evelyn Underhill.[12] The year 1916 saw publication of his book, *Essays in Orthodoxy*, in which Quick was not content "to restate but to explain the creeds, not to put up an apologetic defense but to explore and to dig deeper into the field."[13]

He had ecumenical interests also, attending both the Lausanne and Jerusalem conferences. It seems somewhat strange, then, that in the early 1940s, when it came to the debate concerning the proposals that led to the creation of the Church of South

India, Quick remained silent. The Anglo-Catholic wing of the church was vigorously opposed to this ecumenical scheme. Perhaps Quick's silence had something to do with the war, perhaps also with his failing health. However, Paul Lucas seems firm in his judgment here: "Quick could have provided a saner version of the Catholic vision of the Church and saved Anglo-Catholicism by his sympathetic criticism from a shameful chapter which soured its life for a generation."[14] The Church of South India was something entirely new in the ecumenical era of the twentieth century. Anglican fears of doctrinal and ecclesial reductionism were understandable, if ill founded.

Quick was a theologian who did not recognize an infinite distance between the pulpit and the study: "With Quick's books it is only a short step from the library to the pulpit, from the study to the place where prayer is attempted."[15] This does not mean that his theology, any more than his preaching, was positivistic or overly pious. "There is about all of Quick's work an interrogative style. He is always questing and questioning...."[16] The same interrogative style, pursued more intensely, may be found in Quick's colleague and friend at Oxford, Donald M. Mackinnon, the subject of chapter seven.

The Christian Sacraments

Quick's first great book was *The Christian Sacraments*, and it is to this book we shall turn for an appreciation of his eucharistic theology.[17] He makes a fundamental distinction in this book between instrumentality and significance. The former he associates with Catholicism, the latter with Protestantism. In the Catholic understanding, sacraments are instruments by which God acts upon human beings and our world. In the Protestant understanding, sacraments are symbols signifying a meaning by which we are enabled to grasp some part of the truth. If we approach the question through the scholastic adage, *sacramenta causant significando*, "the sacraments cause [grace] by signifying," the Catholic emphasis is on *causant*, the Protestant on *significando*. Quick, however, maintains that if either is held at the expense of the other, distortion occurs. In this observation we may see him holding together Anglo-Catholic and Evangelical approaches to the sacraments, reflecting also the wider *oikumene*, and in some respects anticipating David Tracy's treatment of the analogical (Catholic) and dialectical (Protestant) forms of the Christian imagination.[18]

The theological distortion results from a failure to grasp that Jesus Christ himself is *the* primordial sacrament of God. Among Roman Catholics the sacramentality of Christ is a notion that gained currency during and after Vatican II, especially as a result of the work of Semmelroth, Schillebeeckx, and Rahner. But in its essence the idea in its twentieth-century expression—for it is deeply rooted in the tradition—is anticipated by Oliver Quick. Christ is *the* sacrament, "in all the good realities of time and space the Divine Logos express[ing] Himself and active towards us."[19] The reality of God approaches us in unparalleled and unique expression in the person of the Lord, so that Christ is *the* sacrament of the unseen God. At the same time, Christ's sacramentality extends upward, so to speak. "As Jesus Christ Himself is the perfect sacrament of created being, so in the light of that one sacrament the Church appears as the sacrament of human society...."[20] Quick's Christology bears more than a family resemblance to that of Karl Rahner, Christ as both and simultaneously the unique point of God's condescension toward creation, and the unique point of creation's upward striving toward the mystery of God. In the economy of the church, the Eucharist is the very center of both movements.

The Eucharist

"The Eucharist to the Christian is the culminating point of all sacramental rites."[21] This has been a central conviction of the Christian tradition for two thousand years, even though it has been articulated in quite different ways at different times. The Eucharist is *the* dominical sacrament par excellence. The reason for this is that in this sacramental rite "[t]he Christian believes that he takes into himself the very life which makes him one with God."[22] The repetition of the rite is not only psychological, that is, serving to remind us of the stupendous fact that God is drawing humankind into the closest possible union of intimacy with himself. The repetition is also ontological in that through the Eucharist God is effecting this union with himself. God is always inviting and enabling this union. God satisfies our human thirst for him in ways known only to God, but the tradition's central conviction is that the Eucharist is the very center because in that center the Giver becomes the Gift. Thus, "[i]n it there must be a real presence of the Lord different from that which is found in any other sacrament."[23]

The basis of the Eucharist is, of course, found in the narratives of the New Testament, St. Paul and the gospels. Writing in the 1920s Quick is well aware of the growing critical approaches to the New Testament. He recognizes scholarly disputes concerning the actual words Jesus used, and he is equally aware of the historical-theological debates as to how those words are to be understood. This latter is the debate between scripture and tradition. His position on both issues is very compelling. In respect of the first he concludes that

> to see nothing in eucharistic theology but a problem of higher criticism and exegesis is to make a very dangerous mistake. It is true that all we need for sound doctrine is to draw out the full implications of our Lord's words and acts. But these implications cannot be drawn out or appreciated if we refuse the help which the subsequent reflection and experience of Christians alone can provide.[24]

With skillful analogues, mainly from the realm of literary criticism, Quick shows that words, especially what might be termed "classical" words, are always more than they appear to mean. This is true of both individuals and of texts. Applied to the eucharistic words of the Lord, the excess of eucharistic meaning emerges under the guiding impulse of the Holy Spirit as one generation after another repeats and reflects upon the eucharistic rite:

> that one great purpose of the sending of the Holy Spirit was to enable us to exhibit ever freshly the riches of meaning which were latent in what our Lord said and did upon earth.[25]

31

The Spirit, working in and through the cumulative generations of the church, leads Christians into a more complete understanding of the entire event of Jesus—words, deeds, and paschal mystery.

The two aspects of eucharistic doctrine that engage Quick above all others are eucharistic sacrifice and presence, the dominant and debated eucharistic doctrines since the Reformation. Quick believes that they are inseparably connected, "that the two are really one."

> Christ died for us so that he might live in us. And his life in us manifests itself in that same activity of self-sacrifice which he in his own person perfectly fulfilled.[26]

The incarnation and the atonement are indissoluble, not only in the continuous narratives of the gospels. They are, by that very fact, the performance in space and time, in the history of Jesus of Nazareth, of the eternal self-donation of the Son to the Father in the heart of the Trinity. Our Lord's free oblation of himself throughout the entirety of his life, his giving of himself in word and parable, in healing both persons and the cosmos, comes to its unique and climactic expression in his giving himself over to death. His death is the highest point of this eternal trinitarian narrative as it is played out in history, the history of Jesus, and, through the Eucharist, our history too. This is how Quick puts it:

> The life of the Son of God is an eternal self-offering to the Father. It was through the Eternal Spirit of his deity that the Lord offered up himself in the flesh of his manhood upon the Cross. But, if so, the activity of his heavenly life is ever one with that of offering. And, inasmuch as the offering of the Son includes our manhood, the communication of his life to us joins us with him in his sacrifice, so that in us and through us, as we receive power to follow in his steps, he is ever afresh, yet ever as one in act, offering up manhood before the throne. The Eucharist then is truly a sacrifice. For it is the perpetual externalization in human ritual of the self-offering of Christ, which was once for all in fact externalized on

Calvary, but is ever real in the inward and heavenly sphere.[27]

Quick's understanding holds the best of the eucharistic tradition together—the Catholic emphasis on the eucharistic sacrifice and the Reformation emphasis on the unique sacrifice of Calvary. What often gets overlooked in theological polemic is that both are rooted in the inner trinitarian dynamic. We might say that in and through regular participation in the Eucharist we are being *christified*, and since christification eternally and historically is marked by sacrificial self-gift, our christification is so marked also. For Quick this is not only high theology, but has practical implications. For example, he makes the point that it is Christ's self-sacrifice in the Eucharist that is the basis and fundament for our prayer for others: "Our prayers at the Eucharist are of special avail, if and because through the eucharistic action the power of Christ's self-offering *reproduces itself in us*."[28] If this is what the Eucharist as sacrifice is accomplishing in the church, it can only be because Christ-as-Eucharist is, in fact, really present in the entire action.

Quick discusses very fairly, albeit briefly, the various theories of eucharistic presence, especially in the last five hundred years: transubstantiation, consubstantiation, virtualism, receptionism. He shows how they both succeed and fail in explicating the mystery of Christ's presence. Properly understood, he maintains that the intentionality of each, for the first two objective and for the latter two subjective appreciations of what is nonetheless *presence*, is closer than is usually understood: "There is as little ground for an accusation of magic in the one case, as there is for an accusation of 'subjectivism' in the other."[29] Why do such accusations occur at all? Quick provides his response to the question, but leaves it somewhat undeveloped. It has to do with human prejudice.

> The mere fact of [the real presence's] historical association with Romanism constitutes of course not a reason but a prejudice; and prejudices no doubt are always influential.[30]

In some measure, at least, the converse may also be said, and the ecumenical movement, in which Quick was a participant, is at great pains to dispel prejudices on both sides of the divide, not least through Faith and Order's 1982 paper, *Baptism, Eucharist and Ministry*.

The eucharistic theory of Will Spens, described earlier, is taken to task by Quick, although "it contains so much which we value and cordially accept." Spens's theory of transvaluation insists that the reality of physical objects is so thoroughly constituted by their value and meaning for persons that an object may be defined as "a persisting complex of opportunities of experience." Among other things, Spens is attempting to move away from what he takes to be a static view of reality that would undermine the vitality and dynamism of the eucharistic presence of Christ. Understood positively, Quick endorses the symbolic side of the theory. The significance of the eucharistic gifts is such that we must value them as Christ's presence in some such way as Spens describes. So far, so good. But the eucharistic gifts may not be thought of as conventional symbols, as "divine" coinage through consecration for Spens. There is more to a sacrament and to the Eucharist than that. The more is that, above and beyond the "significant" aspect of the reality, it achieves something, it does something. This refers in traditional terms to the *ex opere operato* dimension of the sacrament. Something is actually and objectively happening into which the communicating subject is drawn. This is divinization, the operation of grace, God's uniting us with himself. This may be overlooked by Spens, albeit unintentionally, in the conceptual language he uses to describe it, but there can be no doubt, as we have already seen in the section dealing with Spens, that his approach to eucharistic presence is very much in line with the broad Catholic tradition. The communicant, for Quick, believes that

> in so far as he receives the sacraments with a pure faith and a right intention, God will use them to bestow upon him infinitely more than at present he can feel or know. And this is his comfort when sensible devotion fails.[31]

Thus far, Quick's eucharistic theology may be described as creatively Catholic in the best sense of that term.

However, when it comes to the reserved sacrament, there are difficulties. Quick is entirely accurate when he says:

> All arguments for the legitimacy of [eucharistic] Devotions depend upon the affirmation that whatever the consecrated elements are within the eucharistic rite, that they continue to be outside it.[32]

He affirms later, "The communion [of those unable to be present for the Eucharist itself] is in reality simply a postponed part of the eucharistic act; and in it the reserved elements, without further consecration, have to the full that heavenly use and meaning which the eucharistic action gives." Given Quick's ontology of the Eucharist as expressed here, one would think that he would be open to the traditional apparatus of eucharistic devotions, but he is not. The reserved Eucharist ought to be reverently guarded and preserved for communion, but without devotional practices. In point of fact, Will Spens—whose theory of eucharistic presence, "transvaluation," Quick finds wanting because it may give rise to subjectivism of one kind or another—is in favor of eucharistic devotions, thus following through on his eucharistic ontology. The failure to do likewise, it seems to me, undermines Quick's eucharistic ontology. If the reserved elements have that heavenly use and meaning, if they are sacramentally Christ present, that ontology demands the devotional attitude, the adoration due to Christ. Further, one might add that these very acts of devotion have no more purpose than that of the eucharistic action itself, that is, to draw communicants into further graceful union with Christ, in God.

Conclusion

Will Spens and Oliver Quick together show both the richness of Anglican eucharistic theology in the earlier part of the twentieth century, but they seem to me to do more. They also establish that unified faith convictions about the Eucharist may be expressed in different philosophical terminology. They witness to the reality that unity and uniformity are not synonymous.

Notes

1. Philip Snow, "Spens, Sir William (Will)," in E. T. Williams and C. S. Nicholls, eds., *The Dictionary of National Biography* (Oxford: Oxford University Press, 1981), 971.

2. Will Spens, "The Eucharist," in Edward G. Selwyn, ed., *Essays Catholic and Critical*, 3rd ed. (London: S.P.C.K., 1958), 428–29. The book was first published in 1926, and the third edition makes no change to the original essay by Spens.

3. Ibid., 430.

4. Ibid., 431.

5. Ibid.

6. Ibid., 432.

7. Ibid., 438.

8. Ibid., 441.

9. Ibid., 442.

10. Ibid.

11. Leonard Hodgson, "Quick, Oliver Chase," in L. G. Wickham Legg and E. T. Williams, eds., *The Dictionary of National Biography*, 1941–1950 (Oxford: Oxford University Press, 1959), 702.

12. The article was published in *The Journal of Theological Studies*, 1912.

13. Paul Lucas, "Oliver Quick," *Theology* 96 (1993): 5.

14. Ibid., 13.

15. Ibid., 15.

16. Ibid., 14.

17. Oliver C. Quick, *The Christian Sacraments* (London: Nisbet, 1927).

18. See David Tracy, *The Analogical Imagination* (New York: Crossroad, 1981).

19. Quick, *The Christian Sacraments*, 112.

20. Ibid.

21. Ibid., 185.

22. Ibid., 186.

23. Ibid., 187.

24. Ibid., 187–88.

25. Ibid., 190.

26. Ibid., 195.

27. Ibid., 196–97.

28. Ibid., 197, emphasis added.

29. Ibid., 203.

30. Ibid., 206.

31. Ibid., 215.

32. Ibid., 218.

Chapter 4
DOM GREGORY DIX

Gregory Dix (1901–52) was born into an Anglo-Catholic family as George Eglinton Alston Dix on October 4, 1901, in Woolwich, London. He took the name Gregory upon entering religious life as a Benedictine later on. He went up to the University of Oxford, Merton College, in 1920, specializing in history. During this period he became friends with Christopher Butler, who would become a Catholic and a theologian in his own right, as well as abbot of Downside, and then auxiliary bishop of Westminster. During their Oxford days, neither Dix nor Butler would have known that they would both become Benedictines, Dix as an Anglican and Butler as a Catholic. Ordained a priest in 1924, Dix was a lecturer in modern history at Oxford for the next two years. In 1926 he left academic life to join the Anglican community at Pershore near Worcester, which later moved to Nashdom, closer to London. Many years later on the occasion of receiving the DD at Oxford, Dix found himself dining in the company of his former tutor in history, now Professor Garrod. Dix was well known for his wit, which could be acerbic at times, and the story goes that Professor Garrod remarked to him during the meal, "You haven't improved a bit, Dix, since you became a monk." Dom Gregory responded, "I didn't become a monk to improve." To this Garrod said, "So why did you become a monk?" "I became a monk," Gregory answered, "to slow down the deterioration."[1] Dix did not take solemn vows until 1941. One of the reasons for the delay of final vows had to do with the pull of Rome.

From time to time Dom Gregory felt the urge to go over to the Roman Catholic Church, as so many others had done, but he remained in the Church of England as a witness to the religious life and to its longer "Catholic" tradition. He corresponded with the English Jesuit theologian, Maurice Bevenot, about his dilemma, and from one of his letters to Father Bevenot we feel something of Dix's pain and candor:

> I know perfectly well the apparent hopelessness of it, the perversity of it, as it must seem to you—to set out to restore an Anglican Church with its "no-Popery" past, almost inextricably entangled with a mere assertion of National Sovereignty, to the bosom of a Roman Church which virtually denies its existence as a church. It is "cracked" and quixotic and chimerical and everything else you like to call it.[2]

His friendship with Bevenot was to continue. Between them in the late 1930s they initiated informal ecumenical conversations, conversations that involved some of the Jesuit theological faculty at Heythrop College in Oxfordshire and on the Anglican side theologians of the caliber of Eric Mascall (discussed in the next chapter), Lionel Thornton, and Gabriel Hebert. The object was to get to know each other better. From today's standpoint in ecumenism that may not seem much, but it needs to be recalled that in 1928 Pope Pius XI published his encyclical, *Mortalium animos.* This encyclical showed no appreciation for the young ecumenical movement, and the tenor of the Vatican's approach to ecumenism is humorously but not unfairly summarized by Eamon Duffy as follows: "Come in slowly with your hands above your head."[3] Dix was to remain a passionate supporter of Christian unity all his life.

Theologically Dix was well read and could hold his own. Versed in Thomism much like Mascall, he was also read in continental theology. When he came to write *The Shape of the Liturgy,* he could make the claim:

> With the exception of three series of Origen's *Homilies* I have read every sentence of every Christian author extant from the period before Nicaea, most of it probably eight or a dozen times or oftener.[4]

And, of course, the texts were read in the original Greek or Latin. In 1937 he published his text and translation of Hippolytus of Rome's *Apostolic Tradition*, the document that gives us the most comprehensive sense of the liturgy in the third Christian century. The patristic scholar and theologian, Henry Chadwick, who endorsed Dix's achievement, revised this with some corrections and the book remains in print after seventy years as of this writing.[5]

Dix published books on Christian initiation, ministry in the early church, and Anglican orders. However, his most famous and influential theological contribution was *The Shape of the Liturgy*, arguably the greatest piece of Anglican liturgical writing in the twentieth century.

The Eucharist

The Shape of the Liturgy was published in 1945.[6] Dix notes that the "action" of our Lord in the Last Supper narratives of the New Testament was sevenfold: that Christ (1) took bread, (2) "gave thanks" over it, (3) broke it, (4) distributed it, uttering certain words, (5) took a cup, (6) "gave thanks" over it, and (7) gave it over to his disciples, again saying certain words. He reduced this sevenfold action to what he made famous as the fourfold action of the Eucharist: taking, blessing, breaking bread, giving bread and wine. Each of these four actions he associated directly with part of the eucharistic celebration. Thus, "taking" was equal to the offertory; "blessing" to the eucharistic prayer; "breaking" to the fraction; and "giving" to communion. Furthermore, he claimed that "[i]n that form and in that order these four actions constituted the absolutely invariable nucleus of every eucharistic rite known to us throughout antiquity from the Euphrates to Gaul."[7] While there is an obvious, and to no small extent a demonstrable continuity between this fourfold action and the Eucharist of every time and place, nevertheless, contemporary liturgical scholars say that Dix may have pressed it too far.

Dix believes that the Last Supper was a *chaburah*/fellowship meal rather than a Passover meal, as presumed in the Synoptic accounts. Historical issues such as these are finally insoluble given the state of our evidence. What is important is that the meal had and continued to develop Passover connotations. Sometimes, Dom Gregory's patristic references, which are many, are made to do too much. Monsignor James D. Crichton, the late English Catholic pastoral liturgist, remarks, "Where I could check a few of his references I found his translations sometimes said more than the texts."[8] Criticisms like these are important for an accurate assessment of Dom Gregory's achievement in *The Shape of the Liturgy*, but they ought not to detract from the fundament of his eucharistic understanding.

Dom Gregory takes a rather negative view of the medieval period of eucharistic development. He took the view that the decline in communion and the multiplication of Masses created a situation in which eucharistic spirituality became very individualistic. "The old corporate worship of the eucharist is declining into a mere focus for the subjective devotion of each separate worshipper in the isolation of his own mind."[9] There is more than a grain of truth in this judgment. In Dom Gregory's view these medieval eucharistic deficits and developments paved the way, in part, for the Reformation: "And I believe that it can be shewn that in all their mistakes the Reformers were the victims—as they were the products—of the medieval deformations they opposed."[10] However, this recognition did not make of Dix an advocate of the Reformation. His opposition to Archbishop Thomas Cranmer's deviations from the Catholic eucharistic tradition was both constant and strong. He considers Cranmer an out-and-out Zwinglian.[11]

The heart of the eucharistic prayer, for Dix, is the *anamnesis/*memorial of the paschal mystery. It is the proper understanding of this notion that will help assuage traditional Protestant fears about understanding the Eucharist in sacrificial terms. The Eucharist as the *anamnesis/*memorial of Christ's unique sacrifice on the cross does not repeat that sacrifice. This is how Dom Gregory puts it:

> It is not quite easy to represent accurately in English, words like "remembrance" or "memorial" having for us a connotation of something itself *absent*, which is only mentally recollected. But in the Scriptures of both the Old and the New Testament, *anamnesis* and the cognate

verb have the sense of "re-calling" or "re-presenting" before God an event in the past, so that it becomes *here and now operative by its effects....*As the *anamnesis* of the passion, the eucharist is perpetually *creative* of the church, which is the fruit of that passion.[12]

In summary form, the Eucharist makes the church.

The insight that the Eucharist is in this sense the *anamnesis/memorial* is neither unique to Dix nor did it originate with him, but the influence it gained as a result of *The Shape of the Liturgy* has helped it become part of the stock-in-trade of liturgical and ecumenical theologians today.

Dom Gregory had a special fondness for the eucharistic hymn, *Adoro Te*, attributed to St. Thomas Aquinas, and a great love for the Blessed Sacrament. Simon Bailey compares Aquinas and Dix in these words:

> There is an echo in Gregory of that great "Angelic Doctor" of the Church who with his monumental intellect yet composed this intensely devout eucharistic poem. Theirs were minds that longed to pray as well as to think.[13]

He said of the last two verses of the *Adoro Te* that they "squeezed your heart out." Bailey comments beautifully:

> In between all the other complicated motives and issues of his life there was a man in Gregory kneeling with "his heart squeezed out" before the Blessed Sacrament.[14]

This image captures Gregory Dix, the priest, monk, and scholar.

There is a justly celebrated and magnificent passage toward the end of *The Shape of the Liturgy* that speaks both the catholicity of the Eucharist and its deep roots in human history. It is a long passage but a most memorable one:

> [Jesus] had told his friends to do this henceforward with the new meaning "for the *anamnesis*" of him, and they have done it always since. Was ever another command so

obeyed?... And best of all, week by week, and month by month, on a hundred thousand successive Sundays, faithfully, unfailingly, across all the parishes of Christendom, the pastors have done this just to *make the plebs sancta Dei*—the holy common people of God.[15]

There are few passages in the entire history of eucharistic reflection that could match this one for its beauty, its pastoral awareness, its sense of history, and its grasp of the utter centrality of the Eucharist in human affairs. The multiple references, historical and personal, all take root in Dix's fundamental conviction, and the conviction of the entire Catholic eucharistic tradition, that the Eucharist makes the church, that the Eucharist makes "the holy common people of God."

Conclusion

In 1951, just one year before his death, Dom Gregory put together some talks for the three-hour devotional service on Good Friday in New York. These talks were later published, and in one of them he compares the act of dying to the act of adoration. Really, he is speaking of dying and death as preeminently eucharistic:

> [Dying] should be a ritual act, an act of worship—a personal return of life to the God who gave it—to the Lord of all life who is its fount, its master and its end. It should be an act of solemn oblation and worship, an act of acknowledgement, an act of adoration, the pouring out of the whole being to Him whose rightfully it is. Supremely, it is an act of sacrifice to God.[16]

Here is the *ars moriendi*, the art of dying well, at its best, centered on a eucharistic sense of self.

During his last weeks on earth, the Anglican Benedictine, Dom Gregory Dix, was visited by his friend from Oxford days, the Catholic Benedictine, Dom Christopher Butler. While there is no record of their final conversation, it is difficult to imagine both

Benedictines not talking about the meaning of their common Benedictine vocation. Both would have known the statement in the Rule of St. Benedict: "Let them prefer nothing whatever to Christ; and may He bring us all alike to life everlasting."[17] The life of Dom Gregory Dix, OSB, is a witness to this, and his eucharistic reflection, especially in *The Shape of the Liturgy*, is a reminder to us all of how Christ prefers nothing to us, as it were, and brings us through the Eucharist, himself as gift, to life everlasting.

Notes

1. Reported in Simon Bailey, *A Tactful God: Gregory Dix, Priest, Monk and Scholar* (Leominster, UK: Fowler Wright Books, Ltd., 1995), 25.

2. Cited from Bailey, *A Tactful God*, 48.

3. Eamon Duffy, referring to Pius's encyclical letter *Mortalium animos* in his *Saints and Sinners: A History of the Popes* (New Haven and London: Yale University Press, 1997), 262.

4. Bailey, *A Tactful God*, 151.

5. *The Treatise on the Apostolic Tradition of St. Hippolytus of Rome*, ed. Gregory Dix, reissued with corrections, preface, and bibliography by Henry Chadwick (Ridgefield, CT: Morehouse Publishing, 1968).

6. Gregory Dix, *The Shape of the Liturgy* (London: Dacre Press, 1945). The edition used in this essay is Gregory Dix, *The Shape of the Liturgy*, additional notes by Paul V. Marshall (New York: The Seabury Press, 1982).

7. Ibid., 48.

8. James D. Crichton, *Lights in the Darkness: Forerunners of the Liturgical Movement* (Collegeville, MN: The Liturgical Press, 1996), 198. Pages 94–102 of Crichton's book are given over to an appreciation of Dix.

9. Dix, *The Shape of the Liturgy*, 598.

10. Ibid., 598–99.

11. Ibid., 656.

12. Ibid., 248.

13. Bailey, *A Tactful God*, 80.

14. Ibid., 81.

15. Dix, *The Shape of the Liturgy*, 744.

16. Gregory Dix, *God's Way with Man* (London: Dacre Press, 1954), 73.

17. *The Rule of St. Benedict*, tr. Luke Dysinger, OSB (Trabuco Canyon, CA: Source Books, 1996), 167.

Chapter 5
ERIC LIONEL MASCALL

Eric Lionel Mascall (1905–93), trained originally in mathematics and physics and then in theology, was an Anglican priest and a member of the religious community, the Oratory of the Good Shepherd.[1] For thirty-five years he taught theology at Lincoln Theological College (1937–45), Christ Church, Oxford (1945–62), and finally as professor of historical theology at King's College, the University of London (1962–72). A convinced Anglo-Catholic, Mascall drew upon the theology of St. Thomas Aquinas to provide a defense of Christian metaphysics and natural theology against various alternatives: the attacks of logical positivism, process theology (owing its origins and development to Alfred North Whitehead and Charles Hartshorne), and Barthian revelatory positivism.

Mascall was a Thomist. For some that description relegates Mascall to the category of antiquarianism, but his brand of Thomism was neither slavish nor confined to a rediscovery of the past. He encountered Aquinas as a modern man, with modern interests and questions. Mascall's Thomism was steeped in the text of Thomas himself rather than in the many syntheses and commentaries upon St. Thomas. He told John Macquarrie, an Anglican theologian much admired by Mascall, that when the new Blackfriars Latin-English edition of the *Summa Theologiae* was being published in sixty volumes over a period of several years from 1963 onward, he read and reviewed every single volume.[2] No small accomplishment! Mascall was also most interested in the new and creative versions of Thomist thought commonly referred to as transcendental Thomism. In the prestigious Gifford Lectures that he delivered at Edinburgh in 1970–71 and published as *The Openness of Being*, Mascall devoted two chapters to a critical exposition of the thought of the transcendental Thomists, Marechal, Rahner, Coreth, and Lonergan.[3]

His works, *Theology and the Gospel of Christ*[4] and *Whatever Happened to the Human Mind?*[5], establish Mascall's ongoing engagement with crucial issues in Christian doctrine. In these books he showed his heartfelt concern for the ongoing vitality of the Anglican contribution to theology. His plea in his own words was for

> a recovery among Anglicans of Christian theology in the strict and classical sense of "the Science of God," as a living and growing intellectual activity organically rooted in the Christian tradition and consciously operating within the worshipping and redemptive community which is the Body of Christ.[6]

A fine synthesis of Eric Mascall's eucharistic theology is to be found in his book, *Corpus Christi*.[7] It provides us with insight into Anglican eucharistic theology, almost entirely consonant with Catholic eucharistic theology, and almost two decades before the Anglican-Roman Catholic Agreed Statement on the Eucharist in 1971.

Corpus Christi covers some ecclesiological topics as well as the Eucharist, but these are not our concern here. From the range of issues Mascall discusses we shall select the following: the eucharistic canon, the eucharistic sacrifice, the eucharistic presence, adoration and benediction, and the Eucharist and the order of creation.

The Eucharistic Canon

Mascall was not a liturgical theologian but, guided by his friend the Anglican liturgist Arthur H. Couratin, he had various reflections to offer on the eucharistic canon from the viewpoint of a systematic theologian. Showing himself aware of the various interpretations of *anamnesis*/memorial Mascall immediately comes down on the side of the traditional Catholic understanding: "The Eucharist of the Church is not either a commemoration or a dramatic imitation of what was done at the Last Supper; it is *the same thing*."[8] Relying upon the exhaustive analysis of Dom Gregory Dix's

The Shape of the Liturgy, he arrives at the four-action shape of the earliest eucharistic liturgies, that is to say that Christ:

1. took the bread and the cup;

2. blessed the bread and the cup;

3. broke the bread;

4. gave the bread and the cup.

These four actions are represented in the four great acts of the church's liturgies:

1. the offertory;

2. the *sursum corda/* "Lift up your hearts" leading into the canon;

3. the fraction or breaking of the bread;

4. the communion.

It is more than noticing a simple and straightforward parallel between the action of Christ and the action of the church. As Mascall puts it, "the Eucharist is nothing else than Christ's own action in his Body the Church."[9] The ontological bond, we might say the indissoluble bond between Christ and the church, is the foundation for all sacramental activity. The Eucharist is not something the church does as a discrete subject. The church is not a discrete subject but rather the sacramental manifestation of Christ. "It is the act of Christ in the *Corpus mysticum.*"[10]

At the heart of the canon lies the narrative of the institution of the Eucharist by Jesus Christ our Lord, and at the heart of that narrative lie the eucharistic words first spoken at the Last Supper, "This is my body.... This is my blood." We know these words as the consecration. Mascall turns his attention to "the moment of consecration." He recognizes that this has been something of a "vexed question" in theology. His approach is in many ways quite straightforward and commonsensical, and represents the tradition of Catholicism. That is to say, the consecration consecrates. This is how Mascall puts it:

> In whatever terms the eucharistic presence is conceived, the fact remains that the elements were formerly ordinary bread and wine and that they are now the body and blood of Christ. Since they are objects in space and time, there must be some instant at which they ceased to be ordinary bread and wine and became the body and blood. To deny the validity of this statement is not a sign that one holds a pure, unsuperstitious and spiritual doctrine of the eucharistic presence; *it is merely a sign that one is suffering from confusion of mind.*[11]

Mascall will have nothing of those reformed theological positions that distance themselves from the moment of eucharistic change. If something is *y*, but it was formerly *x*, the question of the moment or instant of the change is bound to arise. Equally, he judges the practice of the Eastern Church with regard to the "moment of consecration" to be less than adequate. Mascall maintains:

> It seems at any rate easier to associate the change in the elements with the words by which Christ himself declared their true significance than, as has come to be the practice in the Eastern Church, with words of purely ecclesiastical origin.[12]

Mascall is referring here to the epiclesis as an ecclesial creation asking the Holy Spirit to transform the eucharistic elements. His real concern in this context is to secure the reality of Christ's eucharistic presence in the liturgy, and that is admirable. However, he lacks some nuance with regard to the "moment of consecration." The point can be demonstrated that historically there was no attempt to define the "moment of consecration" before the Middle Ages, and that the rise of Scholasticism made for an excessive desire for precision. This is undoubtedly accurate, but Mascall would argue that precision is no bad thing. Precision is not the same as rationalism, and neither Mascall nor his hero St. Thomas could be construed as a rationalist. Mascall was normally open to and appreciative of Orthodox theology, and this lack of subtlety is somewhat surprising in him.

There really is no impasse here. Both East and West believe in the reality of the transformed-consecrated gifts but express this differently. Perhaps the issue may be resolved by maintaining that the entire eucharistic prayer consecrates, but the heart of the eucharistic prayer *qua* prayer is the words of institution, *the* words of consecration.

The Eucharistic Sacrifice

The relation of the Eucharist to the unique sacrifice of Christ on Calvary has been a divisive issue between Catholic and Reformation theologians for the last half millennium. In caricatured terms, Catholics were understood to believe that the Eucharist repeated Calvary, while for Protestants the Eucharist was a memorial of Calvary. Mascall offers us a somewhat more nuanced summary of the caricature of both positions:

> Catholic theologians have generally asserted that while the Eucharist is a repetition of Calvary, it is not a *literal* repetition, while many Protestant theologians have been anxious to insist that while it is a commemoration of Calvary, it is not a *bare* commemoration; but what exactly is involved in a repetition which is not literal and a commemoration which is not bare neither side has found it very easy to explain.[13]

Ecumenical dialogue has taken both sides far beyond this caricature but, at the time *Corpus Christi* was written, this was a definite impasse. Ecumenically ahead of his time, Mascall set out to show especially Catholics that there was a way of looking at eucharistic sacrifice that did not fall prey to this typical caricature.

The key problem for Catholics, as he saw it, was their thinking of the relation between Calvary and the Eucharist "in terms of repetition [that] has led them almost inevitably to seek for some action in the Mass which can be considered as an equivalent of the slaying of our Lord which took place once for all on the Cross."[14] If Catholics could move away from this repetitive view, they would not be open to Protestant criticism.

Mascall's ecumenical synthesis may be summed up in two important points. First, sacrifice is not seen to be synonymous with death. The predominant view of sacrifice has been that its essence lies in the destruction of the victim. Sacrifice as a concept has a much broader base than this, standing for the entire movement of Christ's coming among us and returning to his Father. The sacrifice of Christ begins with the incarnation, reaches its climax on the cross, but is consummated in the resurrection-ascension.[15] Although Mascall does not put it quite like this, one could say that sacrifice, rather than standing for a discrete action as such, represents the characteristic action of the Divine Communion, the Trinity. "God is Love," says St. John (1 John 4:16), and sacrifice is Love-in-action. Sacrifice is the ec-centric—literally, "out of the center"—pouring out of the self for the other, an outpouring even unto death (John 15:13).

Second, the Eucharist is sacramentally significant of the unique sacrifice of Christ on the cross. Mascall insists that the Eucharist is *the* sign of that unique sacrifice of Christ. He summarizes superbly his point of view as follows:

> The sacrificial character of the Mass does not consist in its being an event which happens to Christ after his Ascension and which in some way repeats or imitates his death, but in its being the means by which the whole sacrificial action of Christ, centred in the Cross and culminating in the Ascension, is made sacramentally present in his Church. It is not a repetition of the sacrifice, nor is it the completion of the sacrifice.... The Mass is not part of the sacrifice; it just *is* the sacrifice—sacramentally.[16]

No hint of repetition here, but a fully articulate understanding of sacrament/sign, without the reductionist presuppositions that so often come in its wake. This is close to the understanding of the Windsor Agreed Statement on the Eucharist, some decades down the road.

The Eucharistic Presence

In many ways the issue of the eucharistic presence of Christ has been just as divisive as eucharistic sacrifice in the last five hundred years between Catholicism and the Reformation tradition. Mascall stands squarely within a Catholic understanding of the Eucharist, but in *Corpus Christi* his concern is not to articulate this understanding in a comprehensive fashion. His focus is in fact quite narrow. He fixes on the words of the Lord in John 6:54: "Those who eat my flesh and drink my blood have eternal life, and I will raise them up on the last day." Here is no invitation to a spiritual relation with Christ by faith, a standard Protestant interpretation of the text. Very sharply Mascall comments: "This is not soul communing with soul, it is men feeding upon a man."[17] Christ is claiming that those who *feed on him* have eternal life and will be raised up.

Theologians have tended to fall into a false spiritualizing language about this eucharistic feeding. Some, operating with a questionable soul-body dualism and assuming that "only the soul matters," have concluded that the Eucharist is about the sanctification and salvation of the soul. In this view the human person is divided into two parts: a body requiring natural nutrition and a soul requiring supernatural nutrition. The more correct view is provided by Mascall:

> Just as the whole man, in his unity of body and soul, is strengthened and refreshed by bread and wine for the achievement of his natural end as a citizen of this world, so the whole man, in his unity of body and soul, is strengthened and refreshed by the Body and Blood of Christ for the achievement of his supernatural end as a member of the Body of Christ.[18]

Adoration and Benediction

Given the theological perspective of Archbishop Thomas Cranmer and also of the 1559 Book of Common Prayer described in chapter one, adoration and benediction of the Blessed Sacrament would seem in principle ruled out among Anglicans. For the most part that is probably true. However, Eric Mascall makes a very good case for not only the appropriateness but also the importance of devotion to the Blessed Sacrament.

He takes up the widespread Anglican viewpoint that the reserved Eucharist should be used for the purpose of holy communion and for that purpose alone. He believes not only that such a view is "impossibly sophisticated" but also that it is unnecessarily confusing to the ordinary churchgoer.

> The facts about the Eucharist which bear directly upon the life and worship of the ordinary Christian must surely be simple and direct, and I cannot imagine him being anything but hopelessly confused if he is told that his Lord and Saviour is present in the reserved Sacrament but that no notice must be taken of his presence because he is there only for the purpose of communion.[19]

Really, Mascall is inferring that failure on the part of the faithful to give due notice to the eucharistic presence of Christ in the reserved sacrament leads logically and theologically to an erosion of belief in that eucharistic presence. Of course, Mascall was talking to his fellow Anglicans in 1953, but contemporary Catholics could also benefit from heeding his approach.

In the above quotation the curious phrase was used by Mascall "the facts about the Eucharist." What "facts"? The fundamental facts about the Eucharist are its being both public and central, not a private object of devotion, but the gift of Christ to the church. So central is the Eucharist to the church that its *publicity*, to use Mascall's term, must be expressed in a strong way in the design of a church and in its worship. Architectural arrangements within the church building should invite the faithful to see that devotion to the reserved sacrament is not to be misconstrued as an optional exercise in piety. Rather, the placement of the tabernacle should visibly teach that eucharistic devotion is to be understood within the context of the church's corporate life and liturgy.[20]

As an advocate of Benediction, Mascall recognizes in this devotion that the blessing with the sacred host reminds us that "in our relation with God, it is he, and not we, who is the primary agent and takes the initiative."[21] It is thus a reminder that in his relationships with us God is always ahead, God always has the initiative. The utter priority of grace is upheld. To underscore the importance of Benediction he suggests that the Blessed Sacrament should be housed in a prominent place—writing before Vatican II, Mascall actually suggests upon the high altar—and further that "regularly some form of devotion to the Eucharistic Presence should be held, if possible when the main body of the congregation is assembled."[22] While Mascall's location of the tabernacle in 1953 would differ from contemporary Catholic liturgical provision, his theological perspective on the tabernacle and the reserved sacrament is identical with that of the Catholic Church.

The Eucharist and the Order of Creation

Under the subheading "Eucharistic Presence" above, it was noted that Mascall was opposed to a "spiritualizing" view of the presence that regarded the Eucharist as feeding and sanctifying the soul, but having nothing to do with the body. This position is developed so that the Eucharist is seen as having to do with the entire order of creation. For Mascall, as for especially the Orthodox and now for many Catholics recovering a cosmic sense of the Eucharist and the liturgy, the human person is "nature's priest." He means by this that the human person is "the focal point in which the material world becomes articulate; he alone, so far as we know, can make a physical noise intelligibly; he alone of material beings can praise God with the intellect and the will."[23] The mute voice of creation reaches its euphonic and symphonic articulation when the human community gathers in worship to praise its Creator.

However, just as human beings are flawed, so too is creation, which also needs to be brought into the sphere of the divine redemption. Human beings need healing; so does creation. This is what the Eucharist achieves. The Eucharist brings before God material objects that are then transformed by the divine acceptance, in that sense overcoming the flaw that is there. In the Eucharist the order of creation reaches by divine grace the shape that God finally intends for it. So, Mascall writes:

> The Eucharist is not only the sacramental and eschato-logical representation of the redeemed community; it is also the sacramental and eschatological representation of the restored and transfigured universe....So, in the Eucharist the final transformation and glorification of the created world is eschatologically anticipated.[24]

Thus, the redeemed material or created order along with its priest, humankind, is presented to the Father in the ascended Christ through the power of the Holy Spirit. The faithful and the cosmos are being drawn up by grace into Christ so that Christ will be "all in all." This was a theme close to his heart. He returned to it in his Boyle Lectures some thirteen years after *Corpus Christi:*

> The Eucharistic rite, which is the source and centre of the Church's life, is both a symbol and a foretaste of the gathering of the human race into Christ and the trans-formation of the material world in him. The conversion of the bread and wine into the Body and Blood of Christ is the symbol and the foretaste of the gathering of the human race into Christ.[25]

This eschatological dimension of the Eucharist, which had fallen into the background in the light of the eucharistic polemics of the last five hundred years, has been retrieved or rediscovered in much contemporary eucharistic theology. A similar emphasis may be found, for example, in the *Catechism of the Catholic Church* (nos. 1402–5). Thus, Mascall not only dealt with such controversial eucharistic topics as sacrifice and presence, but he was aware of the deeper and longer tradition of eucharistic faith, reflection, and devotion.

Conclusion

As an Anglican priest, Eric Mascall loved the liturgy of his church and most especially the Eucharist. He recognized what he took to be the deficits of the eucharistic faith of his Anglican Communion, but he was also critically aware of Catholic eucharistic theology. Mascall was ecumenically minded, treasuring his Anglo-Catholic heritage, yet recognizing the contribution of the Reformation protest. While Eric Mascall's work and contribution may not be on center stage at this time, nevertheless for those willing to find it and engage with it, it is very rewarding. His witness calls not only his Canterbury sisters and brothers to a fuller eucharistic appreciation, but also reminds his Canterbury cousins of the richness of this jewel in the crown, the center of their faith. Let us end with a rich passage from *The Christian Universe:*

> We need more frequent and regular participation in the Eucharist and more frequent and regular reception of Christ's Body and Blood; we need more costing confessions and more eagerly welcomed absolutions. And most of all we need prayer.[26]

Notes

1. For a more complete account of Mascall's life and ministry in the church, see Eric L. Mascall, *Saraband: The Memoirs of E. L. Mascall* (Leominster, UK: Fowler Wright Books, Ltd., 1997).

2. John Macquarrie, *Stubborn Questions in Theology* (London: SCM Press, 2003), 51.

3. Eric L. Mascall, *The Openness of Being* (London: Darton, Longman and Todd, 1971), 59–90.

4. Eric L. Mascall, *Theology and the Gospel of Christ* (London: S.P.C.K., 1977).

5. Eric L. Mascall, *Whatever Happened to the Human Mind?* (London: S.P.C.K., 1980).

6. Ibid., ix.

7. Eric L. Mascall, *Corpus Christi* (London–New York–Toronto: Longmans Green, 1953).

8. Ibid., 52.

9. Ibid., 63.

10. Ibid., 78.

11. Ibid., 73.

12. Ibid., 75.

13. Ibid., 83.

14. Ibid., 85.

15. Ibid., 91.

16. Ibid., 97.

17. Ibid.

18. Ibid., 118.

19. Ibid., 171–72.

20. Ibid., 173–74.

21. Ibid., 175.

22. Ibid., 174.

23. Ibid., 179.

24. Ibid., 180, 185.

25. Eric L. Mascall, *The Christian Universe* (New York: Morehouse Barlow Co., 1965), 163.

26. Ibid., 171.

Chapter 6

W. NORMAN PITTENGER

Norman Pittenger (1905–97), a revered teacher at General Theological Seminary, New York City, spent his thirty years of retirement as senior resident at King's College, the University of Cambridge, England. Richard A. Norris Jr., speaking of Pittenger as a colleague at General Theological Seminary, provides a fine portrait of the scholar and the man:

> Every book one investigated in the library had his name on it, and the terrifying thing was that he remembered not only what he had read, but who had written it, under what title, and in what year. He was, in himself, an entire theological faculty, and, one is bound to own, a more communicative and charming faculty than some one can think of.[1]

Pittenger was a prolific author. His ninetieth and last book was devoted to the Blessed Virgin Mary, and was entitled *Our Lady: The Mother of Jesus in Christian Faith and Devotion*.[2] In a Festschrift for Pittenger, Dean Lawrence Rose emphasized the popularity of his theology: "Many of his writings have been 'popular' in the best possible sense of the word—for people—designed to bring the truth of Christianity out of the cloister or the study and give it currency in the living thought of men and women today."[3]

Pittenger's project of making Christian theology accessible to people led him to a growing appreciation of process thought, especially to the writings of Alfred North Whitehead and Charles Hartshorne. He has presented almost the entire fabric of Christian doctrine in process conceptual categories.[4] Yet it would be incorrect to regard Pittenger as an uncritical and slavish devotee of Whitehead and Hartshorne. He certainly found the process categories of his two mentors as the most adequate for a contemporary articulation of the faith, but his prior allegiance was to the tradition of Christian faith, not to these philosophers. The Catholic theologian, Leo Lefebure, who wrote his doctoral dissertation on Norman Pittenger and Karl Rahner at the University of Chicago, says of Pittenger:

> Pittenger draws heavily upon Whitehead's philosophy in developing his interpretation of Jesus Christ as the classical instance of God's revelation. While he repeatedly expresses his respect and admiration for Whitehead's thought, Pittenger insists that Whitehead's philosophy cannot be simply adopted by Christian theologians without adaptation....Pittenger's concern for the earlier tradition of Christian thought often leads him away from a strictly Whiteheadian position.[5]

That judgment is on target, and we shall see for ourselves that his eucharistic appreciation is not inherently dependent upon the categories of process thought. Pittenger clearly recognizes the priority of the tradition and, indeed, the priority of revelation as he attempts to search out the meaning of Christian life.

Among his many books one will find brief accounts of the Eucharist. For example, in what we might describe as his systematics in miniature, the little 1967 book, *God in Process*, five pages are given over to the Eucharist, and what he says is good.[6] His later 1982 book, *Picturing God*, has a chapter devoted to the liturgical and moral implications of Christian thought with the Eucharist at its heart.[7] Pittenger wrote two books on the Eucharist itself and these will be the main focus of our study: *The Christian Sacrifice: A Study of the Eucharist in the Life of the Christian Church*[8] and *Life as Eucharist*.[9] The former book was published in 1951, and the latter book consists of a series of lectures delivered by Pittenger to Catholic clergy in Amarillo, Texas, in 1972. Lefebure's point is well taken with regard to these books because process categories as such do not play a significant role. It is these two books that will form the substance of our treatment of Pittenger's eucharistic theology.

The Christian Sacrifice

"If the Lord's Supper is dissociated from the Church, and if the Church is dissociated from the faith that Jesus Christ is God in human life for the salvation of men, the Lord's Supper is bound to be misinterpreted and misrepresented."[10] In these words Pittenger acknowledges as the basis for his reflection the strong, ontological connection between Christ, the church, and the Eucharist. When this connection goes unrecognized, the Eucharist is "misinterpreted and misrepresented." A high ecclesiology is necessary, we might say today, for an orthodox and realist appreciation of the Eucharist. The church cannot be seen adequately as a number of like-minded individuals who have a sense of connection with the ideas and the ideals of Jesus Christ. Rather, "[t]he Church is nothing less than Jesus Christ himself, as through the Holy Spirit he is active in the community of believers to make them one in him, as he is one with the Father."[11] He knows this is a "high" view of the church with which some will find difficulty, but nothing less than this high view will do:

> The Christian "thing," then, is not Christ alone. It is Christ known, apprehended, worshipped, served, followed—and, above all, Christ *lived*—in the Body of Christ; it is Christ in, through and with his members.[12]

There is an Augustinian flavor to Pittenger's sentiments as he underscores the united reality of the whole Christ, head and members. It is a flavor found throughout all his work. Nor is the organic connection with Christ new with St. Augustine, but necessarily goes back to the Lord himself. Pittenger's favored gospel passage for demonstrating this organic connection is John 15:1–12, Jesus the True Vine. He acknowledges that advances in the study of the gospels may interpret our Lord's words and meaning rather than providing us with his exact historical utterance. This, however, does nothing to deter his affirmation of the intentional historicity of the passage. He writes:

If we take St. John's Gospel as in any way true to the
essential *idea* of Jesus, even if we agree with recent biblical studies that indicate that it does not represent his
actual *words*, we cannot avoid the central place that inti-
mate interrelatedness, organic wholeness, held in his
mind as to the way in which he and his followers were to
be united.[13]

It is this organic connection between Christ and the church that
enables him to reckon with the obvious criticism of such a high
ecclesiology, namely, the sin and failings of Christ's members in the
church. Because of the real connection between Christ and the
church, with the sap of the vine giving life to the branches, Pittenger
can recognize, on the historical plane, "the astonishing capacity [of
the church] to recover its health."[14] He provides examples in St.
Francis of Assisi helping the medieval church recover its spiritual
health, and of John Wesley's health-giving revival to the Church of
England in the eighteenth century at the onset of the Industrial
Revolution. If Christ is genuinely with the church, in-Spiriting the
church, and being embodied as one with the church, then the life-
giving impetus that comes from his presence in the Spirit will necessarily and finally win out.

There is no doubt in Pittenger's mind that the Eucharist must
be understood as a sacrifice, by way of anticipation at the Last
Supper, and as a memorial subsequently. Pittenger had read Dom
Gregory Dix's *The Shape of the Liturgy*, and so he knew the pros and
cons of scholarly debate about the precise meaning of that supper,
as a Passover meal, or as a fellowship-type meal. He recognized
further that, at the end of the day, this was not especially relevant.
However, whether it is to be understood sacrificially is all too relevant. This is how Pittenger construed the sacrificial dimension of
the Last Supper:

The bread was broken, as his body was to be broken; the
wine was shared, as a participation in the new covenant
that would be brought into being through his sacrifice
for his people. By this action, even before his death itself
had occurred, Jesus set the stamp of sacrificial offering

upon his coming death and made it possible for the members of his "little flock" to share already in that which the death was to accomplish, and which, as the event proved, they were to be instrumental in making available for others as they went out presently to proclaim the crucified Lord who had "brought life and immortality to light through the gospel."[15]

The unique sacrifice of the cross, bringing to climactic completion the entire sacrificial movement of the life of the Incarnate Word, is anticipated by our Lord at the Last Supper. If the biblical skeptics were then to raise questions about the historicity of Christ's injunction, "Do this in memory of me," Pittenger is not fazed. The intention, even if not historically the explicit direction of Jesus, he maintains, was that this fellowship should continue, and that the center of this continuance should be the meal in memorial of him.[16] For Pittenger, the historian would be left with a virtually unanswerable question if this were not the case: Why did the earliest generations of Christians continue to share this eucharistic meal if that intention (if not explicit direction) did not originate in the Lord Jesus, both by word and example, the example of his constant table fellowship, climaxing in the event of the Last Supper? Given his high ecclesiology and Christology, the Eucharist does not remain at the level of the intention of the historical Jesus as a first-century Palestinian Jew, who was marked historically by an inclusive table and fellowship. The Eucharist is the deliberate and intended action of God, an action by means of which humankind might enter into the self-offering of Christ, God Incarnate.[17]

Building upon Dom Gregory Dix's fourfold shape of the Eucharist, Pittenger shows how the authors of the patristic period absorbed and deeply penetrated the meaning of our Lord at the Last Supper. This patristic amplification and penetration of eucharistic meaning, in line with the scriptures, is such that Pittenger concludes that "there is an astonishing consensus in regard to what we have called the eucharistic *idea*....No Eucharist, no Christianity."[18] Without the Eucharist there cannot be Christianity.

He understands this principle, however, not only in terms of the interior life of the church and its worship. The eucharistic sacrifice involves the whole of created reality. It is cosmic in scope. This is how Pittenger puts it:

> Christ, in reconciling men to God, reconciles *the whole created order* to God. The Church, as Christ's Body, appropriately offers to God, in the eucharistic action, the life of all its members, including their work and play as well as their religious life. It offers to God the homes and shops and farms and offices and mills in which his people work. It offers to him the natural world, with its resources and its produce. Indeed, it offers to God, in and by and with the sacrifice of the death of Christ here pleaded, the entire created order that Christ came to redeem.[19]

God is the source and term of all created reality, and is bringing all created reality to its final consummation in Christ. "Through Christ, all things were made," we affirm in the creed. Equally, in Christ, through the Spirit, all things are being transformed, and the very heart of this transformation is the ongoing celebration of the Eucharist. The eucharistic sacrifice for Pittenger is the divinely established mechanism for human and cosmic transformation.

> The very world itself, the materiality of things, as well as history and event in that world, from dust to the *Divine Comedy*, from electron to spiral nebulae, from man's primordial gropings after the good to the struggle for righteousness that is going on in the world today: all this is offered to God, because all this is part of the world God in Christ is bringing to himself, in utter love and with redemptive passion.[20]

In Pittenger's lucid summary, "The Eucharist reproduces in microcosm that which macrocosmically is true of the whole divine operation."[21] The eucharistic sacrifice is the very heart of God's divinizing-transforming action, human and cosmic.

Communion

When the communicant receives the body and blood of Christ in holy communion, Pittenger recognizes here also the cosmic dimension of the sacrament. Communion is obviously communion in the body and blood of Christ, who is both divine and human.

> It is also communion with the entire creation, both above man and below man. The creation above man is included, for man is united with angels and archangels, and with all the company of heaven…the communion of saints is not a vague dream but a realized fact when the Eucharist is offered.[22]

An astute Catholic reader would recognize in Pittenger's words sentiments about the Eucharist superbly expressed in Pope John Paul II's 2003 encyclical letter, *Ecclesia de Eucharistia.*

In this communion of saints, centered in the Eucharist, Mary has her rightful place. Pittenger wrote in his very last book, on Mary: "Thus it is entirely right that in the course of the eucharistic action reference is to be made (however modestly and indirectly) to Mary. She is among those included in the whole company of heaven."[23] Here too the final section of *Ecclesia de Eucharistia,* entitled "At the School of Mary, Woman of the Eucharist," seems in some measure anticipated in Pittenger's theology. Sometimes Catholics are unaware of the central place Mary holds in the Anglican theological tradition.

Needless to say, the fullness of the communion in Christ awaits the parousia, but the Eucharist is also, as Pittenger notes, the very pledge of what is yet to come. "The first fruits, the earnest of [the kingdom] are here and now, as the eucharistic action takes the worshipper, with his brethren, into heaven itself and there brings him into communion with God in that full and free fashion which is to be the life of the Kingdom."[24] In the Eucharist the final transformation, even eucharistification of the universe is anticipated.

This eucharistic vision cannot make much sense unless Christ is really present in the eucharistic gifts, and Pittenger fully recognizes this. Like Will Spens and Oliver Quick, Pittenger is not a fan of transubstantiation as a philosophical articulation of belief in the eucharistic presence. His philosophical preference, as noted, is for process metaphysics, underscoring becoming over being. The eucharistic presence of Christ for him is "a genuine presence," a genuine presence that goes far beyond a mere figurative presence, typical of Huldrych Zwingli, for example.[25]

Nor is this some temporary presence that ends with the celebration of the Eucharist itself for Pittenger. He recognizes with the tradition that the Eucharist is reserved for the communion of those who are ill. He further recognizes with the tradition that

> the direction of devotion, either privately or in regulated public worship, to the person of Christ, present in his risen humanity through these instruments, is right and proper. For where Christ is, there he is to be worshipped and adored. Hence, the practice of prayers before the reserved sacrament has nothing perverse about it.[26]

Nothing would have saddened Norman Pittenger more than Christians absenting themselves from the Eucharist, something all too prevalent in the England of his declining years. In *Sacrifice* Pittenger lamented the poor quality of answer given to those who do not feel the need to receive the Eucharist. Such answers as those that commend the need for some "spiritual" time in the course of a busy week, or that eucharistic attendance helps and supports the moral life of society are not adequate for him. While there might be an element of truth in these responses, they do not get to the heart of the matter for Pittenger. The heart of the matter for him is this:

> The reason it is not simply desirable but utterly necessary for a Christian to attend not a church service but *one* specific service—the pleading of the Christian Sacrifice—is that historical Christianity is a religion that cannot be known and shared and understood without participation in the eucharistic action. To be a Christian *is* to be a eucharistic man; to be a Christian is to assist at the Christian Sacrifice.[27]

It may be the case that treatment of the Eucharist catechetically, theologically, or homiletically as less than the very center of Christian life has been a contributory factor to diminished practice. The World Council of Churches' document, *Baptism, Eucharist and Ministry* (1982), as it continues to be appreciated and to act as a challenge, especially in the churches of the reformed tradition, may well prove in the long haul to be one of the levers needed to help the entire Christian community rediscover the centrality of the Eucharist, retrieve that traditional conviction that the Eucharist makes the church.

Conclusion

It is a statement of fact that Norman Pittenger, through his many books, was one of the foremost spokespersons for process theology during his long life. Clearly he believed that the categories of Whitehead and Hartshorne offered the best promise for a suasive account of the Christian faith in our times. Yet, it is curious that in his treatment of the Eucharist process categories are not to the fore. Rather, in *The Christian Sacrifice* and *Life as Eucharist* there is a straightforward, doctrinal account of the Eucharist in terms of the history of the tradition. I would like to think that this was a recognition on Pittenger's part of liturgy as primary theology—though probably he would not have expressed himself in that fashion—and, therefore, that even one's most cherished philosophical categories are always secondary.

Notes

1. "A Memorial for W. N. Pittenger," *Anglican Theological Review* 80 (1998): 4.

2. W. Norman Pittenger, *Our Lady: The Mother of Jesus in Christian Faith and Devotion* (London: SCM Press, 1996). See Owen F. Cummings, "A Critical Note on Norman Pittenger's Mariology," *New Blackfriars* 78 (1997): 336–39.

3. R. A. Norris, ed., *Lux in Lumine: Essays to Honor W. Norman Pittenger* (New York: The Seabury Press, 1966), 2.

4. A good introduction to his oeuvre is *Catholic Faith in a Process Perspective* (Maryknoll, NY: Orbis Books, 1981).

5. Leo D. Lefebure, *Toward a Contemporary Wisdom Christology: A Study of Karl Rahner and Norman Pittenger* (Lanham, MD: University Press of America, 1988), 146–47.

6. W. Norman Pittenger, *God in Process* (London: SCM Press, 1967), 80–85.

7. W. Norman Pittenger, *Picturing God* (London: SCM Press, 1982), 100–115.

8. W. Norman Pittenger, *The Christian Sacrifice: A Study of the Eucharist in the Life of the Christian Church* (New York: Oxford University Press, 1951).

9. W. Norman Pittenger, *Life as Eucharist* (Grand Rapids, MI: Eerdmans, 1973).

10. Pittenger, *The Christian Sacrifice*, 4.

11. Ibid., 11.

12. Ibid., 13.

13. Pittenger, *Life as Eucharist*, 12.

14. Ibid., 19.

15. Pittenger, *The Christian Sacrifice*, 36–37.

16. Ibid., 37.

17. Ibid., 40.

18. Ibid., 58.

19. Ibid., 118–19.

20. Pittenger, *Life as Eucharist*, 31–32.

21. Pittenger, *The Christian Sacrifice*, 120.

22. Ibid., 130.

23. Pittenger, *Our Lady*, 47.

24. Pittenger, *The Christian Sacrifice*, 134.

25. Ibid., 146.

26. Ibid., 159.

27. Ibid., 199.

Chapter 7

DONALD M. MACKINNON

Donald Mackenzie Mackinnon was born in Oban, Scotland, in 1913 and died in Aberdeen, Scotland, in 1994. Arguably, Mackinnon was one of the ablest lay theologians of the Anglican Communion, and certainly of the twentieth century. His entire life was spent in academe. After studying at Oxford, he returned home to Scotland in 1936 to become assistant in moral philosophy to Professor A. E. Taylor, in the University of Edinburgh. The following year saw him back in Oxford, Keble College, as fellow and tutor in philosophy. Returning again to Scotland in 1947 Mackinnon was Regius Professor of Moral Philosophy in the University of Aberdeen, where he remained until 1960. In that year and until his retirement in 1978, he was the Norris-Hulse Professor of Divinity in the University of Cambridge. He has been described as "one of the most influential post-war British theologians."[1]

Mackinnon never published anything like a handbook of philosophical or systematic theology. His preference seemed to be for the essay, responding to and commenting upon some issue or question or crisis—moral, political, or theological. A member of the Labour Party in Britain, he spoke out on a number of important sociopolitical issues, not least of which was the question of nuclear weaponry during the cold war years.

Drawing upon wide-ranging interests and competence in moral philosophy, metaphysics, Christian doctrine, and literary criticism, among other things, Mackinnon's penchant was for the question rather than for the immediate or seemingly obvious answer, that is, for the interrogative mode of theological discourse. The searching, interrogatory style does not mean that Mackinnon's theology does not feed the Christian soul, but the feeding often comes in surprising ways. One of the ways is Mackinnon's handling of Holy Scripture. He was not in any recognizable fashion a biblical scholar, but he was well informed in biblical studies. He could surprise in scriptural insight, often left undiscovered and uncommented by the scholars. David Ford, the subject of a later chapter in this book and a student of Mackinnon's at Cambridge in the 1970s, provides us with a fine sense of his teacher's serendipitously enriching scriptural technique:

> One of the striking things about Donald Mackinnon's speaking and writing is the way he interprets the Bible. Frequently a passage is focused on, taken up into a discussion, and shown to be fruitful in ways that go beyond the horizons of most scholarly commentaries.[2]

Good examples are to be found in comments he makes on Matthew 25 and the parable of the prodigal son in Luke 15. First, the allegory of Matthew 25. In the scene of the Last Judgment in St. Matthew, the Son of man, likened to a shepherd, separates the sheep from the goats. Here is Mackinnon's comment:

> On the goats is pronounced the judgment of condemnation, a judgment which they reject, questioning indeed when they saw the Son of Man in need, in sickness, or in captivity, and failed at least to try to meet that need. They are told that in as much as they failed so to serve the least of his brethren they failed to serve him. Similarly, the sheep are as surprised by the judge's commendation of their service as their opposites by the condemnation of their lack at once of perception and response.[3]

Thus far, the comment is not especially noteworthy. It is a straightforward paraphrase of what is there in the narrative. Mackinnon continues to comment in a succinct and splendid sentence:

> There is a supreme irony in this presentation of the final judgment upon the human scene. Both innocent and guilty are ignorant alike of the positive quality of their innocence and the negative infection of their guilt.

Though one might look in vain for such a carefully crafted comment among the professional New Testament scholars, the balance of the sentence may not reveal more than a very careful reader of the passage. But let us now move to the punch line:

> "You did it to me." We tend to think of such service too quickly in terms of response to the claims upon our concern of the old who live alone, the senile, the bedridden, the alcoholics, the methylated-spirit drinkers, the heroin addicts, etc. Yet the parable would warn men particularly against the sort of careful restriction of the service of the Son of Man which would enable them to know, with the kind of exactitude with which for instance the constructional engineer may calculate the allowance he must make for wind-stress in building a bridge over the tidal estuary of a great river, precisely what sorts of action specially qualify to be regarded as service of the Son of Man, what human predicaments especially entitle victims of human cruelty or natural circumstance to be accounted his brethren, *whereas the irony of the parable is a warning against precisely this sort of restriction of the area of his claim and presence, this sort of demarcation of places where his demands encounter us.*[4]

This challenging comment surely goes beyond the horizon of the scholarly commentary to throw light upon this passage that will never seem the same again.

Second, the parable of the prodigal son in Luke 15, or as Mackinnon refers to it, the parable of the two brothers. Our sympathies tend to lie with the brother who has squandered his legacy, and returns home to his father's house repentant, acknowledging his sin. Mackinnon is no devotee of cheap forgiveness, and raises pertinent questions about the son, questions that probably do not occur to many readers, and questions not answered by the text.

> What of the damage that the prodigal had done? What of the women with whom he had consorted? We need not suppose that he had himself corrupted them; no

doubt they were professional prostitutes, who had embraced their profession for the sake of the material rewards it brought them. Yet, in his use of them, he had in some measure connived in their debasement of the currency of their lives.[5]

Just as one is warming to this repentant sinner, perhaps because we recognize too much of ourselves in him, we are brought up short by Mackinnon's further interrogation of the parable. Though nothing may be done to undo the prodigal's connivance in the prostitutes' self-debasement, Mackinnon's interrogative style of the biblical narrative requires us to be distant from any form of cheap forgiveness. Forgiveness is seldom easy, never cheap. He disallows the removal of the uncomfortable ambiguities from the narrative.

Eucharist

Mackinnon was primarily a philosophical theologian and, consequently, wrote little explicitly about the Eucharist. What he did write about the sacrament, however, gives us a good insight not only into his eucharistic appreciation, but also into his theology as such. It is strongly realist and strongly Catholic.

Let us focus on his essay, "Parable and Sacrament," published in 1979, weaving his other brief contributions around it.[6] Following Karl Barth's eschewal of arriving at any "extractable essence of religion," and certainly with regard to Christian faith, Mackinnon recognized with unmistakable clarity the problem of "religion." If one were to think of religion as something of a human achievement leading to a kind of spiritual maturity, one would be misled. This has implications for the Eucharist. Mackinnon writes:

> If eucharistic worship is a strangely dangerous reality, it is so because when effort is made to reckon with its many dimensions we are compelled to see that if it is the place of understanding, it is also the place where misunderstandings of many sorts may assume an obstinate permanence in the life of the spirit.[7]

72

There are no masters of the Spirit because the Spirit masters us, and our appreciation of that mastering is the limited and flawed appreciation of the Creator by the creature. The disciplined cultivation of religion, our cultivated religiosity is, therefore, not without its dangers or ambiguities. In point of fact, the notion of ambiguity, found everywhere in Mackinnon, points up with great consistency our flawed appreciation of the divine. Yet, while flawed wisdom may be the best we have to offer with regard to God, Mackinnon was equally convinced of God's passionate involvement with humankind, "the relentless, almost obsessive quest of the Creator for the creature."[8]

The obsessive divine quest comes to expression in the meals that Jesus is recorded as having in the gospels. These are the meals, especially in St. Luke, that Jesus shares with tax collectors and sinners, with the likes of Zacchaeus, as well as with the likes of Simon the Pharisee. Mackinnon describes the meals in this way:

> [Jesus'] studied refusal to refrain from table-fellowship with those from whom a prophet would surely hold himself aloof, was occasion at once of profound gratitude, and of profound scandal.[9]

Gratitude from the marginal, scandal from those of cultivated religiosity. We may go on to ask, "Were these meals religious, were they sacred events?" In any obvious sense of the question, the answer has to be in the negative. That hardly gets to the root of these meals.

> For though these meals have superficially nothing of a ritual or sacramental character, the invitation to join in them, although perhaps almost casually given, is a sign of the Kingdom of God, a type of the call to the Messianic banquet.[10]

But there is more. As well as these "occasional" meals there are the meals with very large numbers, the accounts of the feeding of the multitudes. Mackinnon follows the above quote with: "In the tapestry of the gospels, [the occasional meals] are necessarily woven

73

together with the obviously very significant narratives of the feedings of the four thousand, and the five thousand." These "miraculous" feedings, however they are to be construed historically, were certainly understood by the evangelists to be sacral events, touching on the deeply sacred reality of the Eucharist. They are like the Johannine signs, inducting the reader into a deeper level of theological appreciation and revelation. The divine self-gift comes into the midst of humankind in the Eucharist, anticipated narratively in the miraculous feedings, woven together with what might be called the implicitly eucharistic accounts of the meals in St. Luke. There is throughout a eucharistic continuum. "The meal in the upper room is the last table-fellowship that Jesus enjoyed with his own. But it is also ritual action and religious performance."[11]

What the Eucharist is, and what the Last Supper was, remain controverted issues. Mackinnon takes a stand, not only disallowing any complete division between the event of the Supper and later eucharistic reflection, but also recognizing in such eucharistic reflection a sure interpretative key to the meaning of the Supper. May we say that Mackinnon weaves the interplay between tradition and scripture in such a suasive fashion that the insights generated go well beyond the Eucharist? At the Last Supper, Christ in blessing the bread and the cup revealed the meaning of his death, revealing its final significance—"he makes himself over to God."[12] That is the meaning of oblation at the Last Supper, on the cross, and in the Eucharist. If one admits the cogency of Mackinnon's position, and that seems to me self-evident here, then traditional and polemical debates about the nature of sacrifice, and the relationship of sacrifice to the Eucharist, recede into the background.

> Quite simply, quite untechnically we say that [in the upper room] he gave himself at once to his Father and to us....What he invests with sacrificial significance...is simply himself, himself as he goes to death.[13]

Systematics and exegesis are here mutually enriched in Mackinnon.

The acknowledgment, for Mackinnon, of a continuum of Jesus' table fellowship through the Last Supper draws into question certain liturgical tendencies and temptations in our own times.

Mackinnon means that our too obvious human penchant for drawing careful boundaries around the sacred, our cultivated religiosity, disallows the fundamental Christian recognition of the relentless quest of the Creator for the creature. Where liturgy and Eucharist become ends in themselves we have effectively marginalized the miraculous presence and activity of God. And so, argues Mackinnon, in typical idiom,

> [w]e need to imbue that which belongs to liturgical tradition with a deeply interrogative quality, compelling questioning of the very substance of the liturgy itself as we have received it....We must learn all that is involved in refusing to say that the dominion of God over his world is manifested here but not there.[14]

Mackinnon is much stronger on the sacrificial dimension of the Eucharist than on the question of the eucharistic presence of Christ. However briefly, this latter is also present in his reflection. This is implicit in such statements as "In the gift of the Eucharist is the gift of the flesh of Jesus,"[15] or "We must agree with the universal and age-long tradition of the Christian Church that what is offered *is* the Body and Blood of Christ."[16] In that *is* may be found what is meant traditionally by "transubstantiation," but not the word. However, it must be pointed out that Mackinnon is not adverse to the language of substance in theology, defending its intelligibility and use, for example, in Christology.

There has been, of course, the obligation to participate in the Eucharist every Sunday. Mackinnon says:

> That may seem a narrowing thing, and indeed it would be, were the Eucharist to be regarded merely as an occasion of spiritual experience, or indeed, as it has sometimes been called, "the greatest of human experiences."[17]

This expression is too close for Mackinnon's comfort to cultivated religiosity, and omits much that is central to being present at the Eucharist. The obligation to be present is an acknowledgment of the Christian's "privilege to make intercession in Christ for all mankind."[18] A Christian is not there a participant in Christ's self-oblation to deepen his own spiritual life, though that intention may be assumed, but to pray on behalf of all people. The Christian exercises through his active participation at the Eucharist a priestly ministry that is his or hers through baptism on behalf of all humankind. There is no private Christianity.

He brings to our attention also the eschatological and cosmic dimensions of the Eucharist, though not at any length. Just as the resurrection of Christ is the harbinger of the resurrection of all at the parousia, so the Eucharist signifies and anticipates the cosmic consummation of all creation.

> When bread and wine are brought to the Christian altar, and become by consecration the Body and Blood of Christ, we see in their transformation the type of the renewal of the natural order....The consecration of the Eucharist is the archetype of the transformation of the whole natural order.[19]

Conclusion

Mackinnon's influence on contemporary British theology is considerable, though not especially in liturgical or sacramental theology. Yet, as is clear, the Eucharist is by no means marginal to his theological concerns. He represents a strong realist position in theology—he remained a consistent and sometimes rather outspoken foe of what he took to be philosophical or theological idealism—where realism goes well beyond but yet has implications for "eucharistic realism."

Notes

1. Kenneth Surin in Kenneth Surin, ed., *Christ, Ethics and Tragedy: Essays in Honour of Donald Mackinnon* (Cambridge: Cambridge University Press, 1989), ix.

2. David F. Ford, "Tragedy and Atonement," in Kenneth Surin, ed., *Christ, Ethics and Tragedy*, 117.

3. The comments are taken from "Parable, Ethics and Metaphysics II," in Mackinnon's Gifford Lectures, *The Problem of Metaphysics* (Cambridge: Cambridge University Press, 1974), 84–87.

4. Ibid., 84–85, emphasis added.

5. Donald M. Mackinnon, *Explorations in Theology 5* (London: SCM Press, 1979), 168.

6. This essay appears in *Explorations in Theology 5* (London: SCM Press, 1979), 166–81.

7. Ibid., 181.

8. Ibid., 169.

9. Ibid., 174.

10. Donald M. Mackinnon, "Sacrament and Common Meal," in Dennis E. Nineham, ed., *Studies in the Gospels* (Oxford: Basil Blackwell, 1967), 201.

11. Ibid., 203.

12. Ibid., 203–4.

13. Donald M. Mackinnon, untitled essay in *Report of the Sixth Anglo-Catholic Congress* (Westminster: Dacre Press, 1948), 132–33.

14. Mackinnon, *Explorations in Theology 5*, 180–81.

15. Donald M. Mackinnon, *The Church of God* (Westminster: Dacre Press, 1940), 69.

16. Ibid., 70, emphasis added.

17. Ibid., 71–72.

18. Ibid., 72.

19. Ibid., 73.

Chapter 8

Formal Statements and the Eucharist: The Doctrine Commissions (1938, 1981) and the Windsor Agreed Statement (1971)

In chapter 3 dealing with Will Spens, reference was made to the 1938 Report of the Doctrine Commission of the Church of England, of which Will Spens had been part. In the present chapter we shall look at this report in more detail concerning the Eucharist, contrast it briefly with the 1981 Report on Doctrine, and finally examine the Anglican-Roman Catholic Windsor Agreed Statement on the Eucharist of 1971.

The Doctrine Commission, 1938

In his "Chairman's Introduction" to "The Report of the Commission on Christian Doctrine Appointed by the Archbishops of Canterbury and York in 1922," William Temple, then archbishop of York, provided an overview of the scheme of the report, giving his attention briefly to individual aspects of doctrine. When he came to the sacraments of the church, he had this to say:

We were still further encouraged by the measure of our agreement upon the Doctrine of the Sacraments. Here there are wide divergences within our Church. But to a

78

great extent they are divergences rather of emphasis than of substance.[1]

It would be fair to say that this has been the traditional view of the matter since the English Reformation, that there are wide divergences, differing in emphasis rather than in substance. Were this study to be extended back to every century prior to the twentieth, Temple's statement would be amply verified. In respect of the Eucharist, Temple went on to say:

> In connexion with the doctrine of the Eucharist we have included more technical discussion than elsewhere, partly because it is through exact thinking that we may most hopefully advance towards unity, but partly also because the mere technical discussion illustrates the difficulties confronting those who would penetrate into this mystery, and may thus deepen our humility in any controversial statement of our own views or reflection on the views of others.[2]

The unity Temple had in mind in this passage, in the light of his own personal commitment to the ecumenical cause, surely goes beyond unity within the Church of England to include the growing awareness of and passion for unity in the still fledgling ecumenical movement. He recognized that, if advance toward unity on both fronts were to proceed, it would demand of the expositor of eucharistic doctrine both accuracy and humility, not least in reflecting on the differing views of others. The accuracy and humility Temple had in mind were, at least in some measure, guaranteed in respect of the Eucharist by the membership on the committee of Will Spens and Oliver Quick.

The ecumenical note struck by Archbishop Temple in his introduction to the Report, is reaffirmed in the body of the text when it comes to the Eucharist.

> The Commission is…united in deploring the tragic consequences of this breach of communion between Christians, and its discussion of the underlying significance of this

79

Sacrament would be disproportionate and academic if it did not recognize the urgency of taking every step through which the full communion of Christian people may rightly be restored.[3]

A very clear and unambiguous statement. When the report proceeds to mention the various terms used of the sacrament, it seems to remain uncomfortable with the term *Mass*, noting that "its revival is a matter upon which there is still a wide and strongly felt difference of opinion in the Church of England."[4] And so, the term *Eucharist* becomes the preferred term, the least controversial term used in the Report. In many ways, the treatment of the Eucharist is very fair, looking to both the Anglo-Catholic and to the Evangelical wings of the church in its recognition of traditional insight.

"A living theology of sacrifice survives in Christianity and we believe that Christianity has here preserved for mankind something which is of permanent value, resting as it does upon some of the deepest intuitions of the human spirit."[5] A most positive note is struck right away in the theology of sacrifice in this fine sentence. The notion of sacrifice is beneficial to the human spirit, and the report acknowledges that while other religions—Islam and Buddhism are named—may have dispensed with it, sacrifice remains fundamental. This is sacrifice understood not in a primitive sense, but "determined by the revelation of God as holy Love," and thus an understanding of sacrifice that has undergone "a progressive interpretation upon ethical and spiritual lines."[6]

Sacrifice is examined in its Old Testament senses, use being made of G. B. Gray's influential work, *Sacrifice in the Old Testament*. In the Old Testament, sacrifice is understood as gift, fellowship meal, propitiation and expiation, and covenant. These various levels of sacrificial meaning form the complex out of which the New Testament authors seek to interpret both the cross and the Eucharist.

The Lord's words at the Last Supper quite definitely relate the death which he was about to undergo with the ritual sacrifices of the Old Testament, and though that death was a judicial murder, carried out by Jews and

Romans, He invested it at the Last Supper with a sacrificial character, representing the love and mercy of God.[7]

The Eucharist is the "commemoration" of that unique "oblation" on the cross, offered once for all, "its institution expressly [pointing] to the death of the Lord."[8]

Given the fact that Will Spens was a member of the Archbishops' Commission on Doctrine from 1922 to 1938, it seems strange that in the 1938 report of the commission, *Doctrine in the Church of England*, in the sections dealing with the Eucharist, there is no mention of his work, though the report is not averse to naming the work of scholars as such. When it comes to the eucharistic presence of Christ, there is a brief treatment of transubstantiation, and then comes this remark:

> Some [Anglican theologians] are content with the use of traditional language to express it; but others, especially in recent years, have felt the need for some restatement of it designed to remove traditional objections; and various suggestions for such restatement have been made....[9]

Though no mention is made of him in so many words, it would be difficult to consider that Will Spens is not in the company of those concerned with restatement.

The union with Christ in the Eucharist is best understood as *koinonia*/communion, going back to that first usage in 1 Corinthians 10:16. It is of such a reality that it affects not only the communion of the individual Christian with Christ, but equally with one's fellow Christians.[10] The Eucharist is able to do that because "[n]o Christian doubts that in some sense Christ is present in holy communion."[11] The issue most controverted since the sixteenth century is *how* that presence is to be understood. We find in the Report the usual stock treatment of the history of "real presence." The Report acknowledges a "special" presence of Christ, but this expression seems so loose as to be of little real help in promoting doctrinal clarity, and yet that appears to be the Anglican position, going back at least to the famous "Response of Bishop Lancelot Andrewes to Cardinal Robert Bellarmine": "We believe no less than you that the presence is real. Concerning the method of that presence, we define nothing rashly...."[12] Thus, the Report concludes, reechoing this sentiment of Andrewes:

> It remains to be said that perhaps the strongest and most characteristic tradition of Anglicanism is to affirm such a real presence of Christ in the Eucharist as enables the faithful communicant both to receive His life as a spiritual gift and to acknowledge Him as the giver, while at the same time the affirmation is combined with a determination to avoid as far as possible all precise, scholastic definitions as to the manner of the giving.[13]

The Doctrine Commission, 1981, *Believing in the Church*

This 1981 Report by the Doctrine Commission of the Church of England is quite different in shape from the 1938 report. The late Robert Runcie, then archbishop of Canterbury, provides a very brief foreword to the Report, but it includes a most enlightening paragraph:

> In recent years we have discovered again in our worship what it means "to do things together." The Commission set itself the task of examining the corporate nature of Faith. This is in itself a necessary corollary to the experience that has come to us in corporate worship.[14]

The Report consists of a wide-ranging series of eleven essays treating of the various dimensions of corporate faith, the essays being written by different theologians of the church. Unlike the 1938 Report, the treatment of doctrine is rather uneven, though very good overall.

There is no separate section on the Eucharist. There may even be a weariness with eucharistic controversy, hinted at in some words of Bishop John Austin Baker. He notes "the tyranny of particular questions" concerning the Eucharist, questions to do especially with the eucharistic presence of Christ. The controverted and confusing responses to this doctrine, according to Baker, "served merely to concentrate attention on this one topic, and to ensure that the Eucharist would breed and perpetuate divisions."[15] These divisions haunt even attempts to reach ecumenical consensus, for example, the 1971 Agreed Statement on the Eucharist from the Anglican-Roman Catholic International Commission. Baker writes, sadly:

> The habit of centuries dies hard; and for all that the 1971 Report...presented the Eucharist in a wide variety of aspects and in a vocabulary that, so far as possible, avoided the polemical associations of the past, it was significantly on this narrow front that misgivings arose, and criticisms, often passionate, were voiced from both sides of the ecclesiastical divide.[16]

There is something absolutely on target in this observation of Bishop Baker, a pervasive ecumenical distrust, born of centuries of not knowing each other. At the same time, it is difficult to see how ecumenical progress can be made without some degree of agreement about precise eucharistic meaning.

There is a fine essay in the Report written by the Old Testament scholar, John Barton, and the liturgist, John Halliburton, entitled "Story and Liturgy."[17] The very title suggests a different approach from 1938. Like Baker these thinkers do not engage divisive aspects of eucharistic doctrine. They turn to the importance of scripture in Christian worship. That very turning may itself indicate not only a traditional Anglican locus of theology and spirituality, but may also reflect the infinitely greater scriptural awareness and appreciation in the Roman Catholic Church, following the promulgation of *Dei Verbum*, Vatican II's Constitution on Divine Revelation of 1965. It is not simply a greater awareness of Holy Scripture, as if one could thus "know" the story. The "story" is an integral part of the eucharistic celebration. "It may be called doxological, in that the telling of the story is directed not simply to the congregation, as a word from God or from a teaching church, but also to God, as a form of worship."[18] The importance of the Liturgy of the Word was not prominent in the 1938 Report, but it is here.

The Windsor Agreed Statement on the Eucharist, 1971

The Anglican-Roman Catholic International Commission was established in 1966 by Pope Paul VI and the archbishop of Canterbury, Dr. Michael Ramsey, to engage in dialogue toward the goal of full ecclesial unity. Archbishop Ramsey was not the first archbishop of Canterbury to visit the pope since the Reformation. That honor belongs to Archbishop Geoffrey Fisher, who visited Pope John XXIII in 1960, though more in a private capacity than formally as the archbishop of Canterbury.[19] On that occasion Dr. Fisher was received by Pope John XXIII in the pope's private library. Pope Paul VI received Archbishop Ramsey in the Sistine Chapel with these words: "By your coming, you rebuild a bridge, a bridge which for centuries has lain fallen between the Church of Rome and Canterbury."[20] The following day in St. Paul-Outside-the-Walls both men prayed together, sitting side by side, and issued the Common Declaration, committing both churches to work toward unity by setting up theological dialogue based "on the Gospels and the ancient common tradition." The ancient common tradition is the tradition of doctrine, life, and worship prior to the Reformation and, while this may sound like a typical Anglican locution, Archbishop Ramsey later said, "Those were Pope Paul VI's own words, what he thought to be right, and he put those words into the draft himself."[21] Thus was life given to the Anglican-Roman Catholic International Commission (ARCIC).

Its first agreed statement was the 1971 Windsor Statement on the Eucharist, now over thirty years old. In 1979, after some seven years of critique and comment, a set of elucidations on the agreed statement was published. The veteran Anglican ecumenist, Mary Tanner, has grasped the importance of these elucidations:

> They go a long way to providing a necessary explana-tion...of areas in which genuine difficulties have been encountered, showing how important it is for the churches to enter into dialogue with a statement in the convergence to consensus process.[22]

The elucidations deal with questions and issues that have arisen in the wake of the statement to which the drafters of the statement were privy, but not the readers. Critical questions and issues are what arise when one enters into dialogue with an ecumenical, agreed statement. So, in the treatment of the Windsor Statement in this essay, we shall include comment, where pertinent, from the 1979 elucidations.

According to Herbert Ryan, SJ, the American ecumenist, the ARCIC agreed statement on the Eucharist was much easier to write than the subsequent agreed statement on ministry. Why? Because there already existed a broad ecumenical consensus among theologians on the Eucharist, a consensus exemplified in the subjects of some of the last chapters: Mascall, Dix, and Pittenger.[23] The drafters of the Windsor Statement, and not only on the Anglican side, were aware of the great progress that had been made in the study of the Eucharist, overcoming some of the major difficulties that had opened up at the time of the Reformation. But now to the statement itself. The statement consists of two introductory paragraphs, followed by these subheadings: The Mystery of the Eucharist (par. 3–4); the Eucharist and the Sacrifice of Christ (par. 5); the Presence of Christ (par. 6–11); a concluding paragraph (12).

The statement begins with an acknowledgment of the various names that have been given to the Eucharist down through the ages, and then says, "An important stage in progress towards organic unity is a substantial consensus on the purpose and meaning of the eucharist." Kevin McNamara drew attention to the words *purpose and meaning* in this sentence setting out the tone of the document. The words are "not the happiest choice," he maintained, because they "correspond exactly to the terms 'transfinalisation' and 'transignification,'" which terms had been proposed as alternatives for "transubstantiation" in recent Catholic theology and had been found wanting.[24] The warning is well taken, but McNamara seems to be reading more into the statement at this point than the text actually warrants.

Then the statement proceeds to set out, more or less, the methodology expressed by Pope Paul VI in his historic meeting with Archbishop Ramsey: "Our intention has been to seek a deeper understanding of the reality of the eucharist which is consonant with biblical teaching and with the tradition of our common inheritance...."[25] For all practical purposes this seems to mean that scripture and the patristic tradition, areas in which Anglican theologians have excelled, become the wellspring for this deeper understanding. The medieval tradition of eucharistic reflection did not have great appeal for Anglicans in general as we have seen so far, with the exception of theologians like Eric Mascall. Certainly both scripture and the patristic period reflect the common tradition before the Reformation, but this methodology, while eminently helpful, is not free and clear of problems from a Catholic perspective. The basic problem is an ecclesiological one, and has to do with privileging a particular segment of the tradition over others. Scripture, of course, is the sine qua non for the entire tradition of theological reflection. Patristic theology is so rich that it is difficult to conceive of any theological renewal that is not deeply in touch with it. But, if the Holy Spirit is with the church guiding it into all truth, it becomes very difficult to dissociate any period of history from the Spirit's guidance. In point of fact, the medieval period is far richer in eucharistic thought than is often recognized. It is too often exclusively associated with the question of eucharistic presence, what Gary Macy refers to as the "Paschasian" approach to the Eucharist. There is also, following Macy's analysis, the "mystical" approach and the "ecclesiastical" approach.[26] While the mystical approach, associated with the cathedral school of Laon and the school of St. Victor in Paris, focuses on the Eucharist as the sign of the faith and love mystically uniting the Christian with Christ, the ecclesiastical approach, associated especially with the school of Poitiers, emphasizes the ecclesial unity of the whole *communio* of the church. These are not competing but complementary eucharistic insights. Further, the eucharistic reflection of medieval women mystics like Hildegard of Bingen and Mechthild of Magdeburg enlarges our sense of the eucharistic horizon of the Middle Ages.[27] No ecumenical dialogue can cover everything, but to leave out the Middle Ages almost on principle seems very shortsighted indeed. The "tradition of our common inheritance" in fact includes this period also, and it may be argued, though it is not possible here, that the major eucharistic themes of the fathers are continued, albeit with degrees of intensity and difference, in the scholastic, monastic, and incipient vernacular theologies of the Middle Ages.

The very title of the subsection, "The Mystery of the Eucharist," is revealing. It reminds all that this is an event of grace with an excess of meaning, an excess of meaning that reaches into the heart of God, and, therefore, shares in God's ineffability. The first sentences of paragraph 3 underscore the utter priority of God reaching out to us through the Eucharist:

> When his people are gathered at the eucharist to com-
> memorate his saving acts for our redemption, Christ
> makes effective among us the eternal benefits of his vic-
> tory and elicits and renews our response of faith, thanks-
> giving and self-surrender. Christ, through the Holy
> Spirit in the eucharist, builds up the life of the Church,
> strengthens its fellowship and furthers its mission.[28]

Christ elicits and renews our response of faith, and the Holy Spirit upbuilds the church. The Eucharist is an event of grace, and, there-fore, explicitly a trinitarian event. The statement goes against the Western tendency to see the Eucharist as almost an exclusively christological action. It is also emphasized that in the whole action of the Eucharist Christ is encountered as present, offering himself to his people. The statement already signals at this point the man-ifold presence of Christ that will be featured later.

Paragraph 4 goes on to express the eschatological dimension of the Eucharist, that the Eucharist proclaims the Lord's death until he comes in glory.[29] The recognition that the Eucharist is an anticipation of the heavenly banquet, the liturgy of the new Jerusalem, the "antepast of heaven" of Jeremy Taylor, is what is found here. This has not always been an explicit and obvious part of the last five hundred years of eucharistic reflection, due in the main to post-Reformation eucharistic polemics, when Catholics felt obliged to defend eucharistic presence and sacrifice against Protestants. The day of polemics is over. In point of fact, the same eschatological sentiments found in the statement may also be found in Vatican II's Constitution on the Sacred Liturgy (no. 8): "In the earthly liturgy, by way of foretaste, we share in that heavenly liturgy which is celebrated in the holy city of Jerusalem toward which we journey as pilgrims...."[30] Finally, this paragraph strikes the note of mission flowing from the Eucharist: "[W]e are one in commitment not only to Christ and to one another, but also to the mission of the church in the world."[31] The movement of the Eucharist is, as it were, both *intra* and *extra*. It moves us into the trinitarian embrace, and sends us out in mission to the world, working under grace for its transformation.

Subsection II, "The Eucharist and the Sacrifice of Christ," takes us to one of the issues most divisive at the time of the Reformation in the sixteenth century. Rightly or wrongly, Catholics were understood to maintain that the Eucharist repeats the sacrifice of Christ on the cross, while Protestants underlined the uniqueness of that sacrifice and its all-sufficiency. Immediately, then, the statement lays down as axiomatic that "Christ's redeeming death and resurrection took place once for all in history...."[32] This, however, in no wise disconnects the sacrifice of the cross from the Eucharist, because "God has given the Eucharist to his church as a means through which the atoning work of Christ on the cross is proclaimed and made effective in the life of the church."[33] Taking up the biblical notion of "memorial"/anamnesis, the Eucharist is seen as the memorial of "the totality of God's reconciling action in [Christ]." This is not calling to mind an historic event of the past, but the effective proclamation of that event, the re-presentation of that event in the here and now. All of this is very good theology indeed. We have seen it exemplified in the Anglican theologians considered so far.

Is it too parsimonious to say, however, that there is no actual mention of the Eucharist *as* sacrifice, using this explicit language? Perhaps the absence of this language was intended to assuage the anxieties of evangelical Anglicans who may have interpreted that as too much concession to Catholic tradition and theology. But might it have been more explicit and effective to describe the Eucharist as sacrificial, and then go on to point out how that is so, to emphasize that there is no detraction from the absolute value of Christ's sacrificial death on the cross? There can be no denial that serious misunderstanding of the Eucharist as sacrifice occurred at the time of the Reformation. The Reformation protest would be incomprehensible without some degree of misunderstanding and malpractice. It is difficult to see where it came from, at least in terms of theology. Theological authors of the Middle Ages, those whose works taught the sixteenth-century divines, were clear that there is only one sacrifice of Christ, that is, on the cross, and the Mass does not add to that. Perhaps the clearest example is St. Thomas Aquinas: "The sacrifice which is offered every day in the Church is not distinct from that which Christ himself offered, but is a commemoration thereof."[34] The theological tradition, in contrast to practical and local misrepresentations and misunderstandings, seems very consistent on this issue.

If there is some difficulty with calling the Eucharist sacrificial, the last sentence of the statement is quite splendid as it articulates how the church enters into the unique sacrificial offering of Christ:

> In the eucharistic prayer the Church continues to make a perpetual memorial of Christ's death, and his members, united with God and with one another, give thanks for all his mercies, entreat the benefits of his passion on behalf of the whole Church, participate in these benefits and enter into the movement of his self-offering.[35]

In this one dense sentence we see: the priority of God's gracious action; the Eucharist as the "perpetual memorial" of Christ's death; the church as communion, the members of Christ "united with God and with one another" entreating the benefits of his passion on behalf of all; the church being drawn into the movement of Christ's sacrifice. It is the finest sentence in this subsection. Kevin McNamara has captured with accuracy the meaning of this fine sentence when he says: "It is the Cross itself which lays hold [of the faithful] and draws them into a heaven-ward movement whereby, in offering themselves, they also offer Christ to the Father."[36] McNamara's comment, in fact, goes some way to meeting the point made above about describing the Eucharist itself as sacrificial.

In the elucidations, paragraph 5, there is substantial discussion of the word *memorial* (and its cognates), which clarifies in a pleasing way some of the concerns about sacrifice. Interestingly, from a Catholic perspective, the pedigree of the word is traced not only in the Holy Scriptures where as *anamnesis* it is featured in 1 Corinthians

11:24–25 and Luke 22:19, but also in the Council of Trent, session 22, ch. 1, and the General Instruction on the Roman Missal (1970). This helps to assuage Catholic unease.

Subsection III is entitled "The Presence of Christ." The theological realities signified by the last sentence are entirely dependent upon the presence of Christ in the eucharistic gifts. Without the sheer reality of his presence these words are virtually meaningless. At the same time, the paragraph is very clear about the purpose of the eucharistic presence. It is "to transmit the life of the crucified and risen Christ to his body, the church, so that its members may be more fully united with Christ and with one another."[37] The same basic point is expressed in the elucidations, that is to say, that the bread and wine become sacramentally the body and blood of Christ so that the church may become more fully the body of Christ. Then the statement moves into an expression of Christ's manifold eucharistic presence, in a fashion parallel to Vatican II's Constitution on the Sacred Liturgy. This is what the statement avers:

> Christ is present and active, in various ways, in the entire eucharistic celebration. It is the same Lord who through the proclaimed word invites his people to his table, who through his minister presides at that table, and who gives himself sacramentally in the body and blood of his paschal sacrifice.[38]

Turning to the constitution from Vatican II (no. 7), we read: "To accomplish so great a work [of redemption] Christ is always present in his Church, especially in her liturgical celebrations. He is present in the sacrifice of the Mass not only in the person of his minister…but especially under the eucharistic species.… He is present in his word since it is he himself who speaks when the holy Scriptures are read in the Church.…"[39] Setting the two passages alongside one another yields a remarkable coincidence of theological meaning. They are for all practical purposes identical. Paragraph 8 proceeds to emphasize that Christ's eucharistic presence is not dependent upon the faith of the communicant—"it does not depend on the individual's faith in order to be the Lord's real gift of himself to his church"—but it also recognizes that the spiritual fruit for the individual person is appropriated through a lively faith. This nice theological balance between *ex opere operato* and *ex opere operantis* eschews any charge of sacramental magic.

The term *transubstantiation* occurs in a footnote, and is seen as affirming the *that* of Christ's presence, not the *how* of that presence. This explanatory comment on transubstantiation is so accurate and so concise that one wonders why it has been relegated to a footnote. Were it incorporated in the main body of the statement, perhaps the rather lengthy treatment in paragraph 6 of the elucidations would have been unnecessary. As it stands, that part of the elucidations goes to great pains to emphasize that the change in the eucharistic gifts (named as "transubstantiation") has nothing to do with material change: "It does not imply that this *becoming* follows the physical laws of this world."[40] Writing about two years prior to the Windsor Agreed Statement, the Anglican theologian, Maurice Stewart, concluded, "Properly understood, transubstantiation need no longer inspire the horror in Protestant minds which it inspired in the past."[41] Perhaps a footnote is enough for transubstantiation, but it may also reflect a reluctance to struggle at length and ecumenically with a traditionally divisive concept so as to lay aside once and for all its divisiveness.

The Windsor Statement does not consider the reserved sacrament, but this is taken up in the elucidations. There we are reminded that the practice of reserving the Eucharist may be traced back to Justin Martyr, for the communion of the sick and those unable to be present. Immediately the elucidation moves on to the heart of the question, the veneration and adoration of Christ present in the reserved sacrament. With great care, the trinitarian shape of the Eucharist is the basis for what the elucidation has to say about adoration:

> Adoration in the celebration of the eucharist is first and foremost offered to the Father. It is to lead us to the Father that Christ unites us to himself through our receiving of his body and blood. The Christ whom we adore in the Eucharist is Christ glorifying his Father. The movement of all our adoration is to the Father, through, with, and in Christ, in the power of the Spirit.[42]

91

This is very traditional and very helpful. Further, the elucidation acknowledges, citing the Sacred Congregation of Rites' 1967 instruction, *Eucharisticum mysterium,* par. 49, that "[a]ny dissociation of such [eucharistic] devotion from this primary purpose, which is communion in Christ of all his members, is a distortion in eucharistic practice."[43] However, the elucidation concludes that in respect of reverence and adoration for the reserved sacrament there may be "a divergence in matters of practice and in theological judgments relating to them...." One understands the ecumenical sensitivity behind this utterance, but, not to put too fine a point on it, if the eucharistic gifts may be retained for the communion of the sick, what is it that is being retained? If it is indeed the Christ, sacramentally present in those gifts, would not reverence and indeed adoration, in the sense given by the elucidation and noted above, be entirely logical and theological? Finally, one cannot help but feel that the strong support given to the adoration of the reserved sacrament in Mascall and Dix (and other Anglo-Catholics) was perhaps not given its due place at this point. However, having made these comments, it is also important to ask about the legitimate diversity within a united church. This is not an easy question. What constitutes legitimate diversity becomes very complex when one begins to look at actual issues such as eucharistic reservation and devotion. But perhaps the answer is lived rather than thought. When eucharistic devotion is recognized as always flowing from the celebration of the Eucharist and leading back to it, when it is met with a concern for social justice as a moral demand of participation in the Eucharist, when it is not used as a badge of orthodoxy with which to condemn others, then it may well be that its lasting value in the wider church will also be recognized.

Paragraph 10 retrieves yet again the trinitarian shape of eucharistic worship, already noted in paragraph 3:

> Through this prayer of thanksgiving, a word of faith addressed to the Father, the bread and wine become the body and blood of Christ by the action of the Holy Spirit, so that in communion we eat the flesh of Christ and drink his blood.[44]

Once more the eschatological aspect of the Eucharist comes to expression in paragraph 11: "In the eucharistic celebration we anticipate the joys of the age to come...."

The conclusion, paragraph 12, reasserts the point made in the introductory paragraph that substantial consensus has been reached such that on this basis remaining points of disagreement are capable of resolution.[45] This conviction that "substantial" agreement had been reached on the doctrine of the Eucharist was reinforced in the elucidations.

Conclusion

No attempt has been made in this chapter to include the critique of the ARCIC statement on the Eucharist that has come from the official, institutional church. The reason is that it seems to me better to let the text of the Windsor Statement speak for itself within the community of theological and ecumenical dialogue, rather than to preempt this speaking, as it were, by laying down official responses. The conclusion now offers an opportunity to look briefly at the official responses.

At the outset the official Catholic response to the Final Report, including, therefore, the Windsor Statement, states that it "constitutes a significant milestone not only in relations between the Catholic Church and the Anglican Communion but in the ecumenical movement as a whole."[46] The Final Report's importance goes well beyond the boundaries of Catholic-Anglican ecumenical relations. It provides real hope for the ecumenical cause as such. As one would expect, the official Catholic response proceeds to note that there remain outstanding questions between the two communions that demand exploration, such as the complex issue of authority especially in respect of the Petrine ministry and the exercise of papal infallibility. When it comes to the eucharistic presence of Christ, the official response says of both the Windsor Statement and the elucidations that "[t]hey are insufficient...to remove all ambiguity regarding the mode of the real presence which is due to a substantial change in the elements."[47] Criticism was made above of the way in which transubstantiation was handled methodologically, but it is clear that the Windsor Statement intends a very strong and traditional understanding of Christ's eucharistic presence. One wonders how *all* ambiguity about this presence could be removed. It cannot be that the unease has to do with the question of eucharistic reservation and devotion because that is handled explicitly in the next paragraph of the response. This particular feature of the official Catholic response seems to the writer unnecessary.

The Church of England Response is very positive throughout. In respect of sacrifice and the Eucharist it acknowledges that the Windsor Statement could hardly have been more emphatic that Christ's sacrifice on Calvary was unique, once for all.[48] With regard to eucharistic presence we find something similarly positive. It is accepted that ARCIC has represented the eucharistic faith of the Church of England with accuracy, but the official response also notes, as one would expect, that no official "theory of change" in the elements is posited by the church.[49] Where the Church of England response excels, it seems to me, is in pointing out that there is an insufficient connection in the Windsor Statement and the elucidations between the Eucharist and the cosmos. "Concern for the world cannot be an optional extra in our understanding of the eucharist, but rightly belongs as an integral part of our common belief."[50] Sometimes a preoccupation with traditionally divisive issues prevents a fuller recognition of eucharistic theology.

The brief treatment in the Doctrine Commissions' reports is for the most part eminently acceptable to Catholics. Agreement on the Eucharist in the Windsor Statement and elucidations seems so firmly in place in terms of all its essential features, in other words "substantial agreement" has been reached, that it creates a hunger for more appreciative theological treatments of the Eucharist and for final ecclesial union. When we come in future chapters to look at some of the theological contributions *after* the Windsor Statement, we shall see that this hunger continues to grow, and that eucharistic understanding between Canterbury and Rome continues to advance.

Notes

1. *Doctrine in the Church of England* (New York: The Macmillan Company, 1938), 14.

2. Ibid., 15.

3. Ibid., 139.

4. Ibid., 140.

5. Ibid., 142.

6. Ibid., 142, 155.

7. Ibid., 148.

8. Ibid., 150.

9. Ibid., 169.

10. Ibid., 163–64.

11. Ibid., 165.

12. Cited in Paul E. More and Frank L. Cross, eds., *Anglicanism* (New York: The Macmillan Publishing Company, 1957), 464.

13. *Doctrine in the Church of England*, 170–71.

14. *Believing in the Church: The Corporate Nature of Faith (A Report of the Doctrine Commission of the Church of England)* (London: S.P.C.K., 1981), vii.

15. John Austin Baker, "'Carried About by Every Wind?'" in *Believing in the Church*, 270.

16. Ibid.

17. John Barton and John Halliburton, "Story and Liturgy," in *Believing in the Church*, 79–107.

18. Ibid., 83.

19. Mary Cecily Boulding, OP, "Anglican-Roman Catholic Relations Since Vatican II," *The Downside Review* 121 (2003): 27.

20. Peter Hebblethwaite, *Paul VI: The First Modern Pope* (London: HarperCollins, 1993), 461.

21. Dale Coleman, ed., *Michael Ramsey: The Anglican Spirit* (London: S.P.C.K., 1991), 138.

22. Mary Tanner, "ARCIC in the Context of Other Dialogues," in Mark Santer, ed., *Their Lord and Ours: Approaches to Authority, Community and the Unity of the Church* (London: S.P.C.K., 1982), 50.

23. Herbert Ryan, "The Canterbury Statement on Ministry and Ordination," *Worship* 48 (1974): 11.

24. Kevin McNamara, "Towards Consensus on the Eucharist: The Windsor Agreement," in his collection of essays, *Sacrament of Salvation: Studies in the Mystery of Christ and the Church* (Chicago: Franciscan Herald Press, 1981), 103.

25. The statement is available in various ecumenical collections, but here we are following the Anglican-Roman Catholic International Commission, *The Final Report* (London: CTS/S.P.C.K., 1982), 12.

26. Gary Macy, *The Theologies of the Eucharist in the Early Scholastic Period* (Oxford: The Clarendon Press, 1984). See also Owen F. Cummings, *Eucharistic Soundings* (Dublin: Veritas Publications, 1999), 30–40.

27. See Owen F. Cummings, *Mystical Women, Mystical Body* (Portland, OR: The Pastoral Press, 2000), especially pp. 5–49.

28. *The Final Report*, 12.

29. Ibid., 13.

30. Walter M. Abbott, SJ, and Joseph Gallagher, eds., *The Documents of Vatican II* (New York: The America Press, 1966), 141.

31. *The Final Report*, 13.

32. Ibid.

33. Ibid., 13–14.

34. *Summa Theologica*, III, 22.3 ad 2.

35. *The Final Report*, 14.

36. Kevin McNamara, *Sacrament of Salvation*, 107–8.

37. *The Final Report*, 15.

38. Ibid., 23.

39. Abbott and Gallagher, *The Documents of Vatican II*, 140–41.

40. *The Final Report*, 21.

41. Maurice Stewart, "The Eucharist I," in *Directions: Theology in a Changing Church* (Dublin: A.P.C.K., 1970), 104.

42. *The Final Report*, 23.

43. Ibid., 24.

44. Ibid., 16.

45. Ibid.

46. "The Official Roman Catholic Response to the Final Report of ARCIC I," in Jeffrey Gros, E. Rozanne Elder, and Ellen K. Wondra, eds., *Common Witness to the Gospel: Documents on Anglican-Roman Catholic Relations 1983–1995* (Washington, DC: United States Catholic Conference, 1997), 69.

47. Ibid., 74.

48. *Towards a Church of England Response to BEM and ARCIC* (London: CIO Publishing, 1985), 69.

49. Ibid., 73.

50. Ibid., 74.

Chapter 9

EVANGELICAL ANGLICAN EUCHARISTIC THEOLOGY

In 1989 the Anglican priest and theologian Christopher J. Cocksworth presented a doctoral dissertation to the University of Manchester, "Evangelical Eucharistic Thought in the Church of England, with Special Reference to the Period c. 1960–c. 1980." The dissertation was supervised by Drs. Richard Bauckham and Kenneth Stevenson, now Bishop Kenneth Stevenson. The substance of the dissertation was published as *Evangelical Eucharistic Thought in the Church of England*, and represents the clearest and most comprehensive account on its subject at this time.[1]

Evangelicals are rooted and founded in a lived encounter with Jesus Christ, in the scriptures and in the preaching of the word, but Cocksworth points out that "[i]f Evangelicals are Gospel people and Bible people, they must be also, in some sense, Eucharist people."[2] It is to establish how Evangelicals may consider themselves Eucharist people, without losing the marks of their traditional identity, that Cocksworth enters into both history and theology.

Historical Survey Prior to the Twentieth Century

Evangelical Anglicans hail from the revival of the eighteenth century, but also look back to the great reformers, and ultimately to the New Testament for the foundations of their theology. They recognize that the reformers did not simply abandon medieval sacramental theology and practice, so much as they attempted to retrieve "an authentically evangelical form of sacramental experience," or

98

what might be described as the "truly corporate character of the Eucharist."[3] The key question for the reformers was: Is there a real, saving encounter with Christ in the celebration of the Eucharist, and if so, how? The theologies of Luther, Zwingli, and Calvin created the basic grammar within which reformed eucharistic theology was subsequently to be understood.[4] This key question passed into the liturgical reforms and theology of the Church of England, as summarized in the first chapter. Anglicanism developed its own literary genre and fluency within Reformation eucharistic grammar.

> Although faith was still seen as the prerequisite for the Sacrament, and although the Sacrament was still not defined in causal terms *per se,* a higher emphasis was placed on the sacramental media as the means and instruments of God's activity.[5]

In many ways it is best understood as a middle path between Rome and reform.

While the Puritan tradition may be read as in basic agreement with the Anglican tradition of eucharistic reflection, there were some differences, perhaps best understood as at the level of "experiential expectation." What this means is that Puritan zeal for preaching and authentic faith tended to emphasize the priority of scripture and preaching so much that the Eucharist came to be seen as almost dependent on the word, the word of scripture and the word of the preacher. It developed a spirituality separated from sacramental participation. Thus while *in principle* Anglican eucharistic theology proved no major problem for the Puritans, *in practice* the word and preaching so dominated in worship as to make the liturgical celebration of the Eucharist superfluous or redundant. The nonuse of the Eucharist through the preferred place of preaching led gradually and effectively to its being "lost" as central to the tradition for Puritans.

By the mid-eighteenth century the Eucharist was being celebrated very infrequently, perhaps four or five times a year. A revival occurred especially through the ministry of John Wesley, the "father" of Methodism, and other Evangelical leaders who remained within the Church of England.[6] While Wesley had a very definite ontology of the Eucharist, he equally emphasized that it is not simply the Eucharist "out there" so to speak, but the faith relationship with the eucharistic Lord that counts. The Eucharist fed his soul and was the highest channel of Christ's grace. For Wesley the Eucharist was no parasite of the sermon.[7] The Evangelicals who remained in the Church of England recognized generally the evangelizing potential of the Eucharist, but they were utterly opposed to what they considered mechanical formality. The dispositions and the faith of the communicant are all-important, or the Eucharist "does not work." There is, putting in Catholic terms, no *ex opere operato* dimension to the sacrament.

By the first part of the nineteenth century the Evangelical party had become a force to be noticed in the Church of England. Darwinism and a growing liberal intellectual perspective were very real challenges. But it was the rise of Tractarianism in particular that became the major theological challenge to the Evangelicals. In the Oxford movement there was an emphasis on the objectivity of sacramental grace and the mediation of the priestly ministry in the church, both issues with which Evangelicals had traditionally found difficulty. William Goode (1801–68), a contemporary of John Henry Newman, wrote a lengthy study in 1856, *The Nature of Christ's Presence in the Eucharist*, in which he responded to Tractarian theology. For Goode the central issue was not one or another theory of eucharistic presence—transubstantiation, consubstantiation, or whatever—but "between theologies which locate the activity of God either in the external material of the Sacrament or in the internal experience of the receiver."[8] Another prominent Evangelical theologian, Nathaniel Dimock (1825–1909), maintained that "the question of preserving the purity of our Reformed faith is the question of the hour" and set out to demonstrate that Tractarian theology represented a new departure in theology for the Church of England. In the latter part of the nineteenth century Bishop John Charles Ryle (1816–1900) was the leader of the Evangelical party. Writing about the Eucharist he insisted that right reception by the communicant was the issue, not anything to do with the sacrament *ex opere operato*. Cocksworth sums up the Evangelical approach to the Eucharist on the eve of the twentieth century: "It is the paradox of a relatively high potential allowed to the Sacrament but a relatively low place given to it, first in the theological scheme, and second, despite calls for participation, in the practical system."[9]

Historical Survey, 1900–60

Three issues were to dominate Evangelical eucharistic reflection during the first three decades of the new century: the "Letters of Business" of the Royal Commission on Ecclesiastical Discipline (1906); Charles Gore's book, *The Body of Christ*; Walter Frere's critique of the 1662 communion rite and his consequent call for liturgical experimentation. To each of these Cocksworth has an Evangelical respondent: Edmund Knox (1847–1937), W. H. Griffith Thomas (1861–1924), and Thomas Drury (1847–1926).

The Royal Commission, appointed by the Prime Minister A. J. Balfour, in 1904 opened up questions concerning both the liturgical garb of the ministers and a possible revision of the Book of Common Prayer, both issues that may be seen as products of the nineteenth century Tractarian movement. Let us consider Edmund Arbuthnott Knox, bishop of Manchester from 1903 to 1921 and father of the famous Knox brothers, Wilfred and Ronald. The former became a New Testament scholar in the church, and the latter became the prolific Catholic apologist and translator of scripture, Monsignor Ronald Knox. Edmund Knox wrote an account of the Tractarian movement in which we find this contrast between Tractarians and Evangelicals:

> While in the early part of the nineteenth century there was a great revival of religion throughout Europe, that revival took two forms. One, the Evangelical, was progressive, associated with humanitarian reforms and world-wide missionary enterprise; the other, the Tractarian, was reactionary, guided by romanticism and desire to re-establish the rule of the clergy over the laity.[10]

A somewhat one-sided contrast. For Edmund Knox the issues thrown up by the Royal Commission heralded a Romeward direction:

"Vestments mean the Mass, and the Mass means the whole system of Roman theology." Since the Book of Common Prayer established the decisive break with Catholic eucharistic theology, any interference with the rites of that book is theologically very dangerous. There must be no "fatal counter-Reformation," no corruption of the Book of Common Prayer with liturgical vestments and traditions that smack of Roman Catholicism.

Charles Gore's theology of the Eucharist has been presented in chapter 2 of this book. There we noted the critical reaction, but largely the positive critical reaction of the Anglo-Catholic, Eric L. Mascall. The crucial problem in Gore's *The Body of Christ* was for Griffith Thomas his understanding of eucharistic sacrifice. For Gore there is a soteriological continuity between the death of Christ, his glorified condition, and our participation in Christ's glorified humanity in its "completest degree" in the Eucharist. For Griffith Thomas, however, the sacrifice of Christ has to do strictly and almost absolutely with Christ's death alone. Gore's understanding was much too broad and elastic. The conjoining of Christian lives to this unique sacrifice of Christ through the Eucharist was coming close to losing the uniqueness of the cross. The purpose of the Eucharist is to provide a remembrance of the past sacrifice of Christ through revealing the "force and efficacy" of the crucified body and blood. This remembrance may be made in various ways, including of course the Eucharist, but the Eucharist ought not to be seen as the very center of Christian life.

The liturgical scholar, Walter Frere, was in favor of a liturgical reordering of the communion service, especially of the canon. Without going into detail we may simply say that his desire was to make the canon closer, structurally and theologically, to the eucharistic prayers of the greater tradition. One of Frere's suggestions was to move the prayer of oblation into the prayer of consecration. While Drury was in basic agreement with Frere's suggestions, he distrusted any hint of an oblation of the eucharistic elements, substantially maintaining the Reformation protest in this respect.

> It is the whole service…by the whole congregation…that
> the merits of Christ's death is celebrated in the sight of

God, and with earnest prayer that the merits of that sacrifice may be ours.[11]

Drury was in favor of liturgical change, but not of what seemed to
be doctrinal revision. Liturgical change in fact went ahead, and the
revised Book of Common Prayer was presented to Parliament in
1927. After a three-day debate it made its way through the House
of Lords, but in the Commons everything went wrong. The opposition was led by the low churchman and home secretary, Sir
William Joynson-Hicks, utterly committed to the Evangelical
cause. Some years before, in a letter dated January 24, 1924,
Joynson-Hicks had written to the archbishop of Canterbury,
Randall Davidson, about developments in the High Church party,
especially the Anglican-Roman Catholic conversations at Malines
in Belgium (1921–25):

> The best and most direct path along which we may
> approach the question of Christian unity is in the way of
> re-union with our separated brethren at home, and it is
> the strongest condemnation of efforts of this kind to
> secure union with Rome that not only are they
> absolutely futile, for Rome never yields a tittle, but that
> their success would destroy all hope of re-union with our
> brethren of the Free Churches.[12]

Joynson-Hicks spoke strongly against "the adoration of the Blessed
Sacrament" in Parliament, and for the Elizabethan Prayer Book:

> [We] would not wish to be offered a change of doctrine
> and…hate the idea of any alteration being made in that
> one part of the service of all others, the service of Holy
> Communion, which will bring it nearer to the medieval
> ideas which were abolished for us at the time of the
> Reformation.[13]

Aided and abetted by those who beat the irrational "no-popery
drum," including people who knew little or nothing about the subject
of liturgical revision, the new book was defeated. The ecumenically

minded Bishop George Bell describes what happened: "In a single hectic night the House of Commons had apparently destroyed the work of more than twenty years."[14]

While Bishop Bell's judgment is not inaccurate, it does not exhaust what was going ahead, especially among Evangelicals, that is to say, a rediscovery of the Eucharist and its central and necessary place in the life of the church. This came about as a result of non-defensive interaction with Anglo-Catholics and a renewal of scholarly interest. While the concerns of earlier generations of Evangelicals remained, the post-Tractarian negativism began to dissipate. Recognition emerged of the centrality of the Eucharist in the life of the early church. Perhaps more importantly, there was a retrieval of the position of the classic reformers, a unity of word *and* sacrament, and not the former at the expense of the latter. One major consequence of these promising developments was the publication in 1950 of the Evangelical report, *The Fulness of Christ*, commissioned by the archbishops of Canterbury and York. There we read: "Jesus Christ gives himself to men by means of the word and the sacraments."[15]

Historical Survey, 1960–80

In this period Evangelicalism moved to a more self-critical understanding of itself. Cocksworth underscores the fact that this move did not occur in the same degree for all, and for some did not occur at all. We may isolate three aspects of the more critical self-understanding in respect of the Eucharist: involvement in liturgical revision, contributions to ecumenism, and what Cocksworth refers to as "Evangelicals, the Eucharist and Spirituality."

The details of liturgical revision are enormously complex, but basically the revision was from the failed proposal of 1927, through the various experimental series, to the *Alternative Service Book* of 1981. The central issue was the traditional one of the Eucharist understood as sacrifice. While detailed study was done on the biblical, patristic, and Reformation texts and practices, the Evangelical position remained clear. The priesthood of Christ is both unique and exclusive, and he alone can offer his sacrifice to the Father. This sacrificial work of Christ is over, it is finished and complete, and any suggestion of presentation or offering detracts from it. Anything that might possibly blur the distinction between Christ's unique sacrifice and ours undermines the essence of the gospel. Equally clear was Evangelical opposition to the reservation of the Eucharist. At the same time, Evangelicals, who had a deep love for the 1662 communion service, recognized that times were changing and some degree of liturgical revision was necessary. There were, as one would expect, differences of opinion over the scope and expression of the revision, but for the Evangelicals there could be no deviation from the 1662 Book of Common Prayer, largely a re-presentation of the Elizabethan book of 1559. So, there was openness to the necessary liturgical revision but very definite doctrinal boundaries within which it should be conducted and understood.

Ecumenical dialogue and commitment is the next factor that made an impact on Evangelical attitudes. The most obvious move toward organic union in England was between the Church of England and the Methodists. The section on the Eucharist in the 1963 Report of the Conversations between the Church of England and the Methodist Church was composed in the main by a careful statement of Methodist teaching on the Eucharist. Because it was thought that Methodist theology would lie closer to Evangelical Anglican theology, it was generally believed that this Report would be warmly received. It was not. The opposition came not only from established Evangelical theologians like Roger Beckwith, but also from Methodists. Four Methodists on the commission had dissented over various aspects of its eucharistic understanding as representative of Methodism. The Eucharist, of course, was not the only issue. The question of episcopacy as of the *esse* of the church came into play, with the consequent position that nonepiscopal Methodist orders were defective. The upshot of this ecumenical initiative came about in 1969 when the proposed scheme for Anglican-Methodist union was defeated. Nevertheless, one helpful development was what Cocksworth calls "an unlikely alliance" in 1969 between conservative Anglo-Catholics and conservative Evangelicals to sort out their differences in eucharistic theology and in respect of the about-to-fail ecumenical scheme. Eric Mascall and Graham Leonard for the Anglo-Catholics and Colin Buchanan and James Packer for the Evangelicals worked to produce what was published in 1970 as *Growing into Union*. There is a fine paragraph on eucharistic sacrifice in this document that provides us with a sense that however difficult eucharistic theology seemed to be between the two wings of the church, it was not beyond the hope of reconciliation.

> What can we offer at the Eucharist? Not mere bread and wine...not merely the "fruit of our lips"; not merely undefined "spiritual sacrifices"; not ourselves considered apart from Christ; not even ourselves in Christ, if that is seen in separation from our feeding on Christ; but ourselves as appropriated by Christ. If the sacrament is to communicate to us afresh the benefits of Christ's passion, then it must reaffirm quickly that it also communicates to us the demands of it. It may be good liturgically to express our self-offering as responsive to God's grace...but there is no real time sequence to be represented.[16]

When set alongside the history of polemic and misunderstanding on this aspect of eucharistic theology, this is no small advance in joint understanding and agreement. Reformation and Catholic concerns both find a place, and a place inextricably and indissolubly linked together.

When it comes to the Anglican-Roman Catholic International Commission's (ARCIC) "Windsor Agreed Statement on the Eucharist" of 1971, interpreting the Evangelical response is very complex. A deep suspicion of Rome was in place, but the fact that Evangelicals recognized the signs of biblical reformation in the Catholic Church, and the fact of their acceptance of Roman Catholics as fellow Christians, minimal as this might seem today, were clear and generous signs of their openness to self-critical understanding. The Windsor Statement has been examined in chapter 8 of this book. Evangelical Anglicans of the caliber of Colin Buchanan, Julian Charley, and George Carey (former archbishop of Canterbury) found the Windsor Statement acceptable. Here we shall advert to some pertinent comments only of Colin Buchanan, probably the most informed liturgically of the Evangelical defenders of the Windsor Statement. Buchanan, in response to Evangelical critics, made the following statement on the divisive issue of eucharistic sacrifice:

> In the eucharistic prayer the church continues to make a perpetual memorial of Christ's death, and his members, united with God and one another, give thanks for all his mercies, entreats the benefits of his passion on behalf of the whole church, [in communion] participates in these benefits and [in response] enters into the movement of his self-offering.[17]

Similarly, in respect of consecration of the eucharistic gifts, Buchanan encouraged Evangelicals to see the language of being and becoming, traditionally redolent of transubstantiation, as comments on the "use" or "valuation" of the gifts, terms closer to traditional Evangelical positions. Whatever else one might say or add, what is unmistakable is the very definite openness of Buchanan and of the many Evangelicals whose point of view on the Eucharist he so publicly represents.

The Lima Statement, produced by the World Council of Churches in 1982, probably did not have the same impact among Evangelicals as the Windsor Statement. The Lima Statement was a multilateral document, and not bilateral as the Windsor Statement had been, and further, although Roman Catholics fully participated in the Faith and Order division of the World Council of Churches, Evangelicals had many allies, so to speak, in the council. They were not alone vis-à-vis the Lima Statement. Though the document was not without its critics, most especially Roger Beckwith, the Evangelical, Tony Price, on behalf of the Church of England Evangelical Council, stated that "a study and application of [the Lima Statement] could enrich our own [that is, Evangelical] devotion and church life."[18] A sea change is taking place, slowly but really, in a direction characterized by Christopher Cocksworth as a movement away from the Eucharist as primarily "food for thought" to the Eucharist as "the bread of life."[19]

Eucharistic Theology

Christopher Cocksworth sets out the parameters of eucharistic theology for Evangelicals by starting with two key New Testament passages: the road to Emmaus in Luke 24:13–35, and the discourse on the bread of life in John 6:25–59. In the Lukan pericope the risen Christ is recognized "by an interdependent combination of word and act."[20] Christ revealed himself to the two disciples by breaking open the word of Holy Scripture. This "warmed their hearts" but "did not open their eyes." Their eyes were opened when the Lord Jesus "took," "blessed," "broke," and "gave" bread to them (vv. 30–31). The fourfold action of the Eucharist opened the closed eyes, once the closed ears had been opened by the word. He notes how the skillful Lukan narrative, mediating the interdependent function of word and sacrament, has been shaped by the eucharistic experience of the apostolic community, experience that established the inseparability of word and Eucharist.

In a similar fashion, John 6 presents us with an interpenetration of sapiential and sacramental themes. Christ as the Wisdom of God come down from heaven is present to believers, and Christ as the bread of life is truly eaten by believers. The discourse represents Jesus' presence to believers in the preached word and in the Eucharist. Word and Eucharist belong together, just as in Luke 24.

Cocksworth uses a powerful analogy to bring out the interpenetrative and inseparable dimensions of word and Eucharist, drawn from the world of drama. Just as a playwright intends the audience not only to hear the words of the drama, but so to be drawn into it that they really become part of the action, so with the Eucharist. Listening to the word draws us closer to the performance of the eucharistic action. The performance of the Eucharist has about it an ontology, but an ontology concerning which Evangelicals have nothing to fear. It is not an ontology that is already-out-there-now with a value that is entirely independent of the subject for whom it is intended. Perhaps it may be described as a relational ontology. The reality of the Eucharist is real, but its reality cannot be grasped except in relation to the persons-in-communion who form the church, and for whom, in whom, and with whom it exists for the purpose of trinitarian transformation.

[The eucharistic elements] do not merely help the participant to meditate on the life-giving significance of the Cross, they actually mediate that reality to him. The bread has everything to do with the body because Christ has promised that in this context, the material of bread and wine will be the form through which he will give himself to his people and unite them with him in ever increasing degrees of depth.[21]

This relational ontology offers a way into the traditionally difficult issue for Evangelicals, the Eucharist understood sacrificially. While sacrifice in the Eucharist—the traditional Catholic understanding—has been seen in the past as adding something to Christ's unique sacrifice on the cross, the danger is not unilateral, that is, for Catholics only. "There is the corresponding danger [for Evangelicals] that our response in the Eucharist becomes something additional to Christ's sacrificial action in the sense that it is offered to him rather than with him."[22] As well as the reformed vicarious and substitutionary character of the atonement brought by Christ, there is the Catholic inclusive and incorporative character. What Christ has done, by grace he draws us into. Who we are cannot be understood adequately apart from Christ, the Christ sacrificed uniquely once for all, memorialized in the Eucharist. Who we are is relationally bound to the crucified, risen, and ascended Lord. "In this way we may define the Eucharist as the dominically appointed context both for the renewal of our identification with Christ's death and for the intensification of our participation in his life."[23]

Conclusion

One might describe Evangelical eucharistic theology in the twentieth century as a move from controversy to coexistence and not just a passive, grudging coexistence, but an active and ecumenically fruitful coexistence. Catholics must move away from a somewhat exclusive overattention to the Anglo-Catholics in the Anglican Communion and actively engage the Evangelical tradition. Anything less would issue in a reduced understanding of

Anglicanism, and reduced understanding does not augur well for ecumenical rapprochement.

Notes

1. Christopher J. Cocksworth, *Evangelical Eucharistic Thought in the Church of England* (Cambridge: Cambridge University Press, 1993).

2. Ibid., 9.

3. Ibid., 8.

4. For a brief overview, see Owen F. Cummings, *Eucharistic Soundings* (Dublin: Veritas Publications, 1999), 41–51.

5. Cocksworth, *Evangelical Eucharistic Thought in the Church of England,* 40.

6. For a Catholic appreciation of Wesley's eucharistic theology, see Owen F. Cummings, "John Wesley and Eucharistic Ecclesiology," *One in Christ* 35 (1999): 143–51.

7. Cocksworth, *Evangelical Eucharistic Thought in the Church of England,* 66.

8. Ibid., 80.

9. Ibid., 84–85.

10. Edmund Knox, *The Tractarian Movement* (London: Putnam, 1933), 69.

11. Cited in Cocksworth, *Evangelical Eucharistic Thought in the Church of England,* 90–91.

12. Cited in Randle Manwaring, *From Controversy to Co-existence: Evangelicals in the Church of England 1914-1980* (Cambridge: Cambridge University Press, 1985), 30.

13. Cited in Manwaring, *From Controversy to Co-existence,* 32.

14. Cited in Alec R. Vidler, *The Church in an Age of Revolution,* rev. ed., (Harmondsworth: Penguin Books, 1971), 166.

15. Cited in Cocksworth, *Evangelical Eucharistic Thought in the Church of England,* 97.

16. Cited in Cocksworth, *Evangelical Eucharistic Thought in the Church of England,* 141.

17. Cited in Cocksworth, *Evangelical Eucharistic Thought in the Church of England*, 143.

18. Cited in Cocksworth, *Evangelical Eucharistic Thought in the Church of England*, 145.

19. Cited in Cocksworth, *Evangelical Eucharistic Thought in the Church of England*, 152.

20. Cocksworth, *Evangelical Eucharistic Thought in the Church of England*, 181.

21. Ibid., 199.

22. Ibid., 218.

23. Ibid., 221.

Chapter 10

RICHARD P. C. HANSON

The intention throughout has been to help Catholics appreciate the profoundly *Catholic* dimension of Anglican eucharistic thought, and so authors who reflect that dimension are the primary focus of the book. At the same time I want to suggest the primacy of the Eucharist in Christian worship generally, along with the 1982 World Council of Churches' Faith and Order Report, *Baptism, Eucharist and Ministry*. That ecumenical report, in its section on the Eucharist, says:

> As the Eucharist celebrates the Resurrection of Christ, it is appropriate that it should take place at least every Sunday. As it is the new sacramental meal of the people of God, every Christian should be encouraged to receive communion frequently.[1]

The ecumenical affirmation of the primacy of the Eucharist does not, of course, mean that all Christians understand the sacrament in exactly the same way. As we have seen in the previous chapter, the Evangelical wing of the Anglican Communion, more influenced by continental reformed theology, parts from, in varying degrees, the traditional Catholic understanding of the Eucharist. While the late Bishop Richard P. C. Hanson was no Evangelical, he was certainly not lacking in sympathy with Evangelical eucharistic thinking.

The Hanson Brothers

Although this chapter will deal with Richard P. C. Hanson, it would be remiss not to mention his brother, Anthony. The twin brothers Hanson, Richard Patrick Crosland and Anthony Tyrrell, both of Irish origin though born in London in 1916, served the Anglican Communion mainly in England as priests and theologians. Both were educated in arts and theology at the University of Dublin, Trinity College. Although in the early 1970s Anthony produced a small book on the sacraments,[2] he was in the main a New Testament scholar, the greater part of his academic career being spent as head of the Department of Theology in the University of Hull (1963–82).[3] He never lost sight of the broader concerns of the church, however, and, when the Irish School of Ecumenics was first established in Dublin in 1970 under the leadership of the Irish Jesuit, Michael Hurley, it was Anthony Hanson who provided through his department at Hull an academic affiliation for the new establishment.[4] A colleague of Anthony's, Ieuan Ellis, describes the Hull affiliation with the Irish School of Ecumenics:

> One of the most fruitful new developments was our association with the Irish School of Ecumenics, which began in 1972 and resulted in a number of MA and diploma candidates whose examinations and theses we were glad to validate. We were grateful for the opportunity to assist in the launching of such an important ecumenical enterprise, and wished the ISE well when it finally became associated with Trinity College, Dublin, in 1982—an augury of great hope for the future of Ireland and church unity generally.[5]

Long before this venture, Anthony had been involved as a teacher of theology with the Church of South India (1947–59), of which he became a presbyter.

Richard, equally at home in the New Testament and in the world of patristic scholarship—he was awarded the DD for his contribution to the theology of Origen of Alexandria—spent much of his academic career at the University of Nottingham, where he was a colleague and friend of Alan Richardson. Elevated to the episcopate as bishop of Clogher in Ireland, Richard returned to his native land, but not for long. Ireland was going through some of its worst times in the twentieth century, and Richard found the situation extraordinarily difficult. It has been described in this way:

> What in the end made his work impossible was that he found himself increasingly opposed to the very influential Orange Order; after finally making a public attack on it and thereby alienating a large number at least of his laity, who more or less declared a boycott, Richard decided with utmost reluctance that his future lay in England, in academic work.[6]

He resigned as bishop and returned to England where he served as professor of Historical and Contemporary Theology in the University of Manchester until his retirement.

Not less than Anthony was Richard Hanson involved in the cause of Christian unity. In a little book jointly authored with the New Testament scholar Reginald H. Fuller, Richard entered the ecumenical lists. The book was entitled *The Church of Rome: A Dissuasive*, and was designed to be of help to Anglicans or Protestants who might be tempted to go over to Rome.[7] Though it would hardly act as a dissuasive today—it was twelve years before the Second Vatican Council—it displays Richard's interest in, respect for, but differences from Catholic theology and practice. It is there that we shall begin to outline his understanding of the Eucharist.

The Eucharist

Richard Hanson wrote chapters 2, 3, 4, and 6 of *The Church of Rome: A Dissuasive*. Picking up what was often an arrow in the quiver of the Protestant polemicist, Hanson addresses the belief that Roman Catholics practice their faith, especially in attendance at Mass, out of fear. He will have none of it: "The whole argument that Roman Catholics are frightened into loyalty to their Church becomes absurd for anybody who has any extensive acquaintance with Roman Catholic folk."[8] He intends to continue his dissuasive, but it is not a tirade against Catholicism.

The quality of his dissuasive becomes particularly clear in some comments about George Tyrrell, the Irishman who was a member of the English Province of the Society of Jesus and was condemned as a Modernist. After a brief consideration of the difficult details of Tyrrell's life, Hanson concludes: "It was probably right that George Tyrrell should leave the Roman Catholic Church, but that Church quite unnecessarily besmirched its good name in its treatment of him before he ceased to be a Roman Catholic."[9] Argument about the Tyrrell affair, and indeed the interpretation of the phenomenon of Modernism, continues, but we may see here an indication of Richard Hanson's attempt to play fair ecumenically. Hanson intensely disliked what he took to be an abuse of authority, and this is what he found to be the case with George Tyrrell.

It was no less the case in the withholding of the chalice from the laity. He asks the question:

> Is the action of the Roman Catholic Church in withholding the cup from the laity in the sacrament of the Eucharist of no more significance than the custom, which grew up early in the history of the Church, of taking symbolically and not literally our Lord's command to his disciples to wash each other's feet?[10]

Hanson had an esteem for tradition, but he could not abide what he saw as something construed to be traditional that was nothing more than a consequence of the abuse of authority. This, it needs hardly to be said, is an issue positively engaged in the liturgical reforms that came about after Vatican II.

Richard Hanson is equally critical of his own Anglican ecclesial tradition. Recognizing that the Eucharist is central to the church, he laments the loss of the Eucharist in the regular experience of ordinary Christians. Through historical accident or ordinary human sinfulness, the celebration of the Eucharist became irregular in churches of the Reformation tradition, including the Anglican Communion. Though appreciative of efforts to remedy this deficit, Hanson was not particularly optimistic. The number of communicants in proportion to churchgoers did not give great grounds for hope. And that was in 1948!

Hanson's theological methodology may be described as pugnacious, but a pugnacity that was always gracious and fair. Benjamin Drewery is more nuanced in his description of Richard: "Any attempt to 'classify' him would be helplessly inadequate. He was a 'Liberal Catholic/Evangelical'...a 'Broad Churchman' in the 'central tradition,' an 'Anglo-Irish Protestant' whom the 'Protestants' rejected."[11] A similar, broad definition of Richard's theological and ecclesial perspective is offered by his brother Anthony in a context contrasting Anglo-Catholics with Evangelical Anglicans:

> There has been a tendency in the recent past to see that which is distinctively Anglican as exhibited more clearly by Anglo-Catholics than by Evangelicals.... Richard is not, and never has been, an Anglo-Catholic. But neither has he ever been remotely like an Evangelical in the British sense of the term....He is in fact a mere Anglican. Indeed I suspect that he would be happier still to describe himself as a mere Catholic.[12]

I am sure that both Drewery and Anthony Hanson are right in this comprehensive description, but, when it comes to sacramental theology, it is entirely fair to situate Richard on the Evangelical side of the divide.

In 1980 both Hanson brothers published together a book entitled *Reasonable Belief: A Survey of the Christian Faith*.[13] The introduction to the book is revealing of their methodology and general outlook. They considered the work to be a survey of the Christian faith by Anglican theologians. And so doctrinal and other issues that might be considered important or even essential by Christians of other denominations are not tackled. One example is Mariology, because they did not consider it an integral and indispensable part of Christian faith. One wonders about such judgments given that in Vatican II's Constitution on the Church the Blessed Virgin Mary features as the final chapter, and both Hanson brothers were very ecumenically committed. In other words, the conciliar teaching is that Mary is best understood within ecclesiology, and ecclesiology is surely integral and indispensable to Christian faith. However, this is not to say that the book is not ecumenical in import. It is replete with ecumenical references. Indeed, commenting on Vatican II, the authors point out what they see as a most significant gain:

> It is true indeed that the Roman Catholic Church does not yet recognize other churches as full and proper parts of the Catholic Church: but the old exclusive spirit has gone. Co-operation at many levels and friendliness now prevails. Deep friendships between Catholics and Protestants in many and varied situations have been formed. These bonds will not be repudiated.[14]

Nonetheless, it would be fair to say that the book has been written from the standpoint of a critical Evangelical Anglicanism, similar to the earlier work of Richard Hanson. The book is dedicated to Alan Richardson, and it sees itself continuing his theological tradition.

The section on the Eucharist in *Reasonable Belief* is not very long, and shows all the marks of Richard's hand. He notes that "[c]ontroversy has raged round the eucharist in the Church of the West more fiercely than round any other doctrine."[15] No debate there! He recounts the famous dispute over the eucharistic presence of Christ between Luther and Zwingli at the Marburg Colloquy, each reformer insisting on his own understanding of the word is/*est* in "This is my body"/*Hoc est enim corpus meum*. Retrieving the fact that Aramaic, Jesus' own language, has no word for *is* as such, Hanson concludes that "[t]hey were fighting fiercely about a word which Jesus did not use."[16] To say the least, this seems a rather facile remark. Whether Jesus used the word *is* or not, any reading of the text yields the conviction that he intended an identity between himself and the bread and the wine, "my body, my blood." Anything other than this rests on a very forced exegesis. Hanson agrees, but the nature of the identity is what gives him trouble.

On the whole, the tenor of the chapter shows him attempting to distance himself from Catholic eucharistic theology as it has traditionally been expressed. On the other hand, the Eucharist remains central for Hanson. He seems caught between these two positions. What happens in the Eucharist is that the congregation, the communicants, "are brought into the redeeming activity of Christ," and "by means of eating the bread and wine are united again in Christ's life."[17] These words, though one would want to be more precise, certainly articulate Catholic understanding. But then we find Hanson insisting equally that "[w]hat needs to be reduplicated is our part in his act, not his presence in consecrated bread and wine." The problem seems to be that he has failed to develop an adequate understanding of sacramentality, as well as what might be called the integrity of Christ and the church. The integral Christ, head and members of his body, is present when the assembly comes together to celebrate the Eucharist. Christ is not absent, but very present. The deep grammar of the eucharistic prayer suggests that Christ becomes uniquely present as bread and wine, as food, so that that food may be said to be, ontologically but sacramentally, Christ. He seems not to wish to distance himself entirely from this perspective because he emphasizes that in and through the Eucharist we are drawn into Christ's redeeming activity and are united again in Christ's life. How can this be unless Christ somehow *is* present? Is this what he means when he affirms, "In [the Eucharist] we are liable to meet God himself"? The ontology of Christ present in the eucharistic gifts makes the ontology of Christ present, head and members. Hanson exhibits a certain ambivalence, as when he goes on to say: "We have no right nor authority to offer Christ, and if we have priests they are not priests whose function and status are defined in terms of the cult.... We do not control Christ, through a priest or by any other means."[18] The tradition of eucharistic thinking has never suggested that we control Christ, nor that we offer Christ discrete from our being offered with him.

In a very erudite paper in patristic eucharistic theology, Hanson returns to this notion of sacrifice. "We do not offer Christ as a sacrifice for our sins, in the eucharist or on any other occasion. To do that would be inevitably to return to the old, anxious nagging at God which is ultimately a confession of lack of faith."[19] Catholicism does not stand for an anxious nagging at God in the eucharistic sacrifice. It stands for a gracious being drawn into the sacramental re-presentation in the eucharistic act of that unique sacrifice for sin on Mount Calvary. To be sure, Christ is offered, but offered in this integral sense of Christ as head drawing his members into deeper conformity with himself in this re-presentation of his unique self-donation.

If Hanson's eucharistic theology is judged faulty here from a Catholic point of view, it may be, however, that Catholics have contributed to this misunderstanding. It may be that Catholics in word and practice give the impression of an anxious nagging at God, and too seldom articulate in theory and practice a trinitarian eucharistic appreciation: being drawn to the Father, in the Son, through the Holy Spirit. Perhaps without intending to, this failure has fueled Anglican eucharistic theologies such as that of Bishop Richard Hanson.

Notes

1. *Baptism, Eucharist and Ministry* (Faith and Order Paper 111) (Geneva: World Council of Churches, 1982), par. 31.

2. Anthony T. Hanson, *Church, Sacraments and Ministry* (London: S.P.C.K., 1975).

3. See the festschrift, Barry P. Thompson, ed., *Scripture: Meaning and Method. Essays Presented to Anthony Tyrrell Hanson for his Seventieth Birthday* (Hull, UK: Hull University Press, 1987), for details of A. T. Hanson's contributions to theology.

4. Michael Hurley, SJ, acknowledges his debt to Anthony Hanson in his *Christian Unity: An Ecumenical Second Spring?* (Dublin: Veritas Publications, 1998).

5. Ieuan Ellis, "Dedication," in Thompson, ed., *Scripture: Meaning and Method*, xvii.

6. Benjamin Drewery, "A Short Biographical Memoir," in Benjamin Drewery and Richard Bauckham, eds., *Scripture, Tradition and Reason: A Study in the Criteria of Christian Doctrine. Essays in Honour of Richard P. C. Hanson* (Edinburgh: T. & T. Clark, 1988), 7.

7. Richard P. C. Hanson and Reginald H. Fuller, *The Church of Rome: A Dissuasive* (London: SCM Press, 1948).

8. Ibid., 25.

9. Ibid., 37–38.

10. Ibid., 93. He comes back to this very issue in *Reasonable Belief*, 234 (see footnote 13).

11. Drewery, "A Short Biographical Memoir," 7–8.

12. Anthony T. Hanson, "An Account of the Writings of R. P. C. Hanson," in Drewery and Bauckham, eds., *Scripture, Tradition and Reason*, 25.

13. Richard P. C. Hanson and Anthony T. Hanson, *Reasonable Belief: A Survey of the Christian Faith* (Oxford and New York: Oxford University Press, 1980).

14. Ibid., 246.

15. Ibid., 232.

16. Ibid.

17. Ibid., 234.

18. Ibid., 237.

19. Richard P. C. Hanson, *Eucharistic Offering in the Early Church* (Bramcote, Notts.: Grove Books, 1979), 29. This paper was reissued in his *Studies in Christian Antiquity* (Edinburgh: T. & T. Clark, 1985), 83–112.

Chapter 11
DAVID F. FORD

David F. Ford, Regius Professor of Divinity in the University of Cambridge, England, was born in Dublin in 1948. After reading classics at the University of Dublin, Trinity College, he studied theology at Cambridge, with some time at Yale Divinity School, completing his dissertation under the late Donald M. Mackinnon. The work of Karl Barth had never been a forceful influence on theology in England, but it was a major interest of Mackinnon's. Barth was the focus of Ford's research, and his dissertation was published as *Barth and God's Story*.[1] His time at Yale saw the influence on David Ford of two members of the theology faculty, the late Hans Frei and George Lindbeck, key players in postliberal theology.[2]

Ford's first teaching appointment was in the Department of Theology of the University of Birmingham, England, in 1976. One of the senior lecturers in systematic theology in the department was the Reverend Daniel W. Hardy. The two became close theologically and domestically. Ford married Deborah, Hardy's daughter, and both he and his father-in-law produced a very fine book together, *Praising and Knowing God*.[3]

Cooperation in theology was not to be limited to the discipline of systematics. Another colleague in the department was the New Testament and patristic scholar, Frances M. Young. Ford tells us how his collaboration with Young originated: "My favourite verse in the Bible is 2 Cor. 4.6. I once mentioned this to a colleague, Professor Frances Young, and said that some day, perhaps in retirement, I would love to write a book on 2 Corinthians. She went home, re-read the letter, and next morning I found a note in my pigeonhole: 'When do we begin our book on 2 Corinthians?'"[4] Their cooperation was to bear fruit in Frances M. Young and David F. Ford, *Meaning and Truth in 2 Corinthians*.[5]

121

Theology in Praise

Praising and Knowing God is the American title of the book, suggesting the genre of spirituality and prayer. Those, needless to say, are most important issues for Hardy and Ford, but the American title does not convey the dynamic of the book. The English title is *Jubilate: Theology in Praise*, and it conveys much better the thrust of the book: "...praising God, recognizing him as God in feeling, word and action, is a key to the ecology in which right knowledge of God grows...."[6] Ford likes the word *ecology*.[7] A commonplace dictionary definition would yield something like this: "The science of the relationships between organisms and their environments." The word expresses for him the rich and necessary interconnections between a living subject—the individual Christian, the church—and its living and growing environment. It is essentially a dynamic word. And so the key to the ecology of right knowledge of God is praise. The right knowledge of God is mediated through all genuinely praiseworthy events and experiences in life. Nor does this permeative emphasis on praise remain unaware of the dark side. It is not a doxological positivism. The problem of evil and suffering is recognized in all its horror, but the praise of God still remains the ecology for right knowledge of God.

> Evil's historical particularity is met on the cross, and evil's dynamic, spreading overflow through history is met by the Spirit of the resurrected Lord. It is an answer to evil that is essentially practical, taking the form of a call to live in this Spirit and follow the way of the cross, trusting in the vindication of God by God. Praise of God celebrates his identification of himself through the crucifixion and resurrection of Jesus.[8]

Anything less than this perspective concedes too much to the powers of destruction and rests too confidently in the power of reason to sort out all that ails humankind. Christian theodicy is best performed in discipleship, a discipleship the heart of which is praise.

Theology and Worship

"Exploring worship is a way into some of the richest veins of theology."[9] Ford means by this that worship brings into synthesis all the major aspects of Christianity. In the early centuries of the church, it was liturgy that expressed and carried forward the expanded approach to God as Trinity. It was worship that carried all the dimensions of a high Christology. One thinks, for example, of the various hymns to and about Christ that feature in the Pauline letters, for example, Philippians 2:5–11 and Colossians 1:15–20. It is commonly acknowledged by New Testament scholars that passages such as these find their originating context in the liturgy of the earliest Christians.

But Ford does not simply want to draw attention to the historical development of key Christian doctrines through worship. It is not simply a history lesson. There is a first order intensity to the experience of liturgy with which academic theology cannot compete. This is how he puts it:

> [Theology] can use overviews, integrating concepts and systematic interrelations, but it has a more basic need of images, metaphors, and symbols which can shape thinking, imagining, desiring, feeling, and action together. Here theology can come only a poor second to liturgy, poetry, story, music, and architecture.

It is not a matter of abandoning systematic theology as of no consequence. "Theological thought has its own forms of inspired intensity in theory, analysis, commentary, and argument."[10] However, there is a certain primacy to liturgy and worship. We may even say, perhaps—though Ford does not use this terminology —that worship is primary theology. When he lists the various disciplines to which theology can come only a poor second, it is interesting to note that they all come into play in the choreography of liturgy. Story is found in the Liturgy of the Word, the story of salvation, preparing the way for the indwelling of the Word in our midst. Poetry, as the beautiful arrangement of words, creatively crafted, is *the* verbal medium of liturgy, for example, in the Gloria, in the psalms, in the eucharistic prayers. Music has played a substantial role in liturgy in the Jewish-Christian tradition from the time of the First Temple at least. And the shape of the liturgical space, the architecture, provides the ambience for this experience of God's coming to us, to draw us closer to God.

Poetry has been very important to Ford's theology. This is what he writes about poetry:

> The discipline of poetry-writing is a highly-developed, millennia-old way of helping to shape life. It calls the rest of us non-poets to two disciplines in response: to the discipline of high-quality attention to what poets write, including learning some poems by heart; and to comparable dedication to high-quality communication in our own ways.[11]

The acknowledgment of the Triune God whose being overflows into the great plenitude of creation is praise poetry.

Eucharist

"The Eucharist or holy communion or mass or Lord's Supper is probably the ritual most participated in and most discussed in human history...from the beginning of the church the eucharist has been intrinsic to its identity."[12] Despite its being intrinsic to the church, despite, we might say, the recognition that "the Eucharist makes the church," the Eucharist has been, as we have noted, the focus for the abstractions of debate and polemic in the Middle Ages and the Reformation. In some respects the Eucharist has "often been discussed in abstraction from the complex 'ecology' of how the eucharist actually worked as the main taken-for-granted ingredient in shaping the common-sense world of Christianity."[13] Again, we notice the word *ecology*, suggesting powerfully that if the Eucharist is not appreciated in the central dynamic of praise of God as a living and transforming experience, it is but little understood. Ford is interested in the question: What happens soteriologically, what happens to the eucharistically shaped self? He wants to deal

with the Eucharist not so much in the analytic fashion of systematic textbooks, but in its dynamic reality.

It is sheerly impossible to inquire into the actual practice of
every worshiper, but one might inquire into the key concept of the
eucharistic *habitus.* Borrowing from anthropology *habitus* means
something like: "habitual ways of being and behaving, with a reper-
toire of predispositions, tendencies, propensities and inclinations,
all shaped by structures and previous actions."[14] The meaning of
the Eucharist is unfolded, then, not from treatises and textbooks,
however venerable, because inevitably "such accounts in language
alone are abstractions from its complex ecology."[15] When the
Eucharist is understood as flowing out into the entirety of human
life, then its centrality to Christian living is obvious at every level.
There is a "superabundance of meaning," so that one might say
there is a eucharistic economics, a eucharistic politics, a eucharistic
morality, and so forth. There is no area of life that remains
untouched when the Eucharist is engaged. Furthermore, Ford
maintains that the Eucharist is a synthesis of Christian doctrine:
"Each major Christian doctrine can be worked out through it. Each
part of the liturgy can be a lens through which the whole is understood."[16] In a Catholic vein we could say that the primary expression of the hierarchy of truths of the faith, a phrase that gained
currency at Vatican Council II, may be found in the Eucharist.

There is an obedience to the person of Jesus at the heart of the
Eucharist: "Take, eat, drink, do this...." And these imperatives find
their wider context in the crucifixion and resurrection. "There can
be no quick leap across Gethsemane and Calvary."[17] The paschal
mystery of Jesus, in its fullness, provides the *ecology,* to use Ford's
term, of Christian discipleship. Dying to live. "To remember [the
Last Supper] is to be commanded in such a way that to recognize
this death as 'for us' is to find that one's fundamental imperative is
to improvise on it in new situations and so discover an unimagin-
able fullness of life through death."[18] Not only are we baptized into
Christ's death, the pervasive theme of St. Paul to the Romans, but
we are constantly fed a discipline of death in sharing the Eucharist.
Fed by this death-dealing, self-donation of Christ, Christians are
commanded and empowered to live out the paschal mystery appro-
priately and radically in their own life contexts.

This perspective does not leave the church curved in upon the Eucharist, disconnected from the rest of creation. Ford has truly appropriated traditional biblical and patristic themes concerning the Eucharist when he maintains that it may be best understood as *blessing*.

> Perhaps the best summary of what happens in the eucharist is: *the blessing of Jesus Christ*. Blessing is a word whose biblical and traditional use enables us to maintain the priority of God without seeming to diminish humanity or creation. God blesses and is blessed, we bless and are blessed, creation blesses and is blessed, and a glorious ecology of blessing is the climactic vision of the Kingdom of God....The eucharist generates a habitus of blessing and offers a hospitality which incorporates people and the material world by blessing.[19]

Worship and sacraments, with the Eucharist as center, represent "the most explicit embodiment of the unlimited, God-sustained ecology of blessing and being blessed."[20]

The Eucharistic Self

Putting all these elements together, what kind of person is a eucharistic person? How is a Christian a eucharistic person? What is the shape of the eucharistic self? First, "the most embracing description is that a eucharistic self is blessed and blesses."[21] The Christian as eucharistic becomes a source of blessing for others for she has been the recipient of blessing in the Eucharist. Could we take the aphorism of Ford from his earlier work, *Praising and Knowing God*, that "praise is the ecology for growth in right knowledge of God," and turn it around? The Eucharist is the ecology for growth in right knowledge of the other, and so of the Other. The Eucharist "invites and initiates into a eucharistic practice in order to sustain a life of flourishing within the infinite love and joy of God."[22]

Second, just as place is intrinsically bound up with the person, so the eucharistic self is placed.

> Baptism and eucharist are a new placing of the self: under water…and around a table. Inseparable from the water and the table are other people, the community of the face.[23]

The "catholic" placing of the self, the integral placing of the self above all social and racial and national particularities is "given" in the Eucharist (preceded, of course, by baptism). The catholic self is eucharistic because through this unique, graced act of self-donation the person is incorporated into the Divine Communion, as body of Christ and temple of the Spirit.

Third, the eucharistic person is timed. Each person is framed by time as well as place. The Eucharist times those who are church. "A self may be timed by the eucharist."[24] Being timed by the Eucharist frees and liberates the eucharistic person to evaluate his or her time. It can encourage "seeking wisdom about the focusing and distribution of time and energy in the other times with which the self is enmeshed—those, for example, of nature, nation, children, financial markets, television, novels, music, and business organizations."[25] The Eucharist both directs and shapes the eucharistic self in time, and especially at the time of death. Being timed and placed by the Eucharist relativizes death so that the Eucharist is "the normative Christian way of facing suffering and death without letting them have the last word."[26]

Finally, the eucharistic self is commanded. The command is the dominical command: "Do this in memory of me." The repeated doing of the Eucharist creates a eucharistic habitus for the self, described by Ford in these words:

> Repetition after repetition of hearing scripture and its interpretation, of repentance, of intercession and petition, of the kiss of peace, of communion, of praising and thanking, all within a dramatic pattern that slowly becomes second nature: who can tell in advance what sort of self is being shaped year after year as these practices are interwoven thoughtfully with all the rest of life?[27]

Conclusion

Mascall, Dix, and Pittenger wrote about the Eucharist in a different theological genre from David Ford. Ford comes at theology from a perspective that weaves together many interesting and different strands: scripture, poetry, contemporary continental European philosophy and theology, to name but a few of the strands. The freshness of David Ford's approach to theology and to the Eucharist in particular, I hope, is evident. The ec-stasy—literally, standing "outside of"—of praise of God, climaxing in the superabundant meaning of the Eucharist, is full of rich potential for humankind and culture. The transformative power of the Eucharist is constantly underlined by Ford in a most attractive and compelling fashion. At the same time, that this is so is dependent upon the *reality* of the Eucharist, and recognizing that reality takes us into the troubled territory of the questions that our medieval and Reformation forebears agonized over: eucharistic sacrifice, the "real" presence of Christ. Ford deliberately does not enter these troubled waters, and precisely because, important as they are, they are abstracted from the ways in which the Eucharist actually shapes this actual life. Yet, they must be entered. Controversial questions about the Eucharist, if the unity of the church is to be healed, must be engaged. If there was a departure from traditional eucharistic meaning at the time of the Reformation, perhaps that departure as loss needs to be noted. Further, the retrieval of a pre-Reformation perspective in engagement with a contemporary philosophical framework may be the way to do it. In chapter 14 we will discuss Graham Ward, a self-styled "radically orthodox" theologian who tries to do just that.

Notes

1. David F. Ford, *Barth and God's Story*, 2nd ed. (Frankfurt: P. Lang, 1985).

2. For a brief introduction to postliberal theology, see Owen F. Cummings, "Towards a Post-liberal Religious Education," *The Living Light* 28 (1992): 315–24.

3. Daniel W. Hardy and David F. Ford, *Praising and Knowing God,* (Philadelphia: The Westminster Press, 1985). For a sense of the connection between the two men, see David F. Ford, "Introduction: The Architecture of Life with God," in David F. Ford and Dennis L. Stamps, eds., *Essentials of Christian Community: Essays for Daniel W. Hardy* (Edinburgh: T. & T. Clark, 1996), 1–20.

4. David F. Ford, *The Shape of Living* (London: HarperCollins, 1997), 96.

5. Frances M. Young and David F. Ford, *Meaning and Truth in 2 Corinthians* (London: S.P.C.K., 1987).

6. Hardy and Ford, *Praising and Knowing God,* 112.

7. There are fifteen references in the index of subjects to "ecology" in *Praising and Knowing God.*

8. Hardy and Ford, *Praising and Knowing God,* 106. It is also found throughout Ford's later book, *Self and Salvation: Being Transformed* (Cambridge: Cambridge University Press, 1999).

9. David F. Ford, *Theology: A Very Short Introduction* (Oxford: Oxford University Press, 1999), 54. For a similar description of Ford's theology, see Owen F. Cummings, "Christianity as Doxology," *Antiphon: A Journal for Liturgical Renewal* 7 (2002): 7–9.

10. Hardy and Ford, *Praising and Knowing God,* 119.

11. Ford, *The Shape of Living,* 86.

12. David F. Ford, "'Do this': A Eucharistic Self," in *Self and Salvation,* 137.

13. Ford, *Self and Salvation,* 138.

14. Ibid., 140.

15. Ibid., 142.

16. Ibid., 145.

17. Ibid., 147.

18. Ibid., 148.

19. Ibid., 156.

20. David F. Ford, "Why Church?" *Scottish Journal of Theology* 53 (2000): 55.

21. Ford, *Self and Salvation,* 162.

22. Ibid., 163.

23. Ibid.

24. Ibid.

25. Ibid., 163–64.

26. David F. Ford, "L'Arche and Jesus: What Is the Theology?" in Frances M. Young, ed., *Encounter with Mystery: Reflections on L'Arche and Living with Disability* (London: Darton, Longman and Todd, 1997), 87.

27. Ford, *Self and Salvation*, 164.

Chapter 12

KENNETH STEVENSON

Kenneth William Stevenson (born in 1949) was for a time Anglican chaplain to the University of Manchester, England, and taught liturgy in its Faculty of Theology. He has written a number of books on liturgy: on early Christian worship,[1] the Eucharist,[2] marriage.[3] His academic theological interest in the Eucharist goes back at least to his 1975 PhD at the University of Southampton, "The Catholic Apostolic Eucharist." His commitment to liturgy has been not only at the academic level, but also at the practical. He had been a parish priest for a number of years before becoming bishop of Portsmouth. In many ways he exemplifies the Anglican tradition of the scholar-parson, working away at his theology while ministering as a priest in a local community. In this essay, our focus will be on Bishop Stevenson's theology of the Eucharist, excluding for the most part his historical studies of the sacrament.

Eucharistic Presence

In his joint work with the late Henry R. McAdoo, Anglican archbishop of Dublin, *The Mystery of the Eucharist in the Anglican Tradition*, McAdoo deals with the "mystery of presence," while Stevenson focuses on the "mystery of sacrifice." He has not written very much about the eucharistic presence of Christ, though what he has to say about sacrifice is dependent upon a firm and strong grasp of Christ's eucharistic presence.

Bishop Stevenson makes the point that, while the earliest Christians believed firmly in what later generations of Christians came to call "the real presence" of Christ, they had little or no interest in pursuing an intellectual analysis of this faith conviction.

Christ is present, both in the reading and in the preaching of the word and at the table, in the sharing of the bread and wine.... But they were reluctant to *define how* Jesus is present. They would not have understood many of the tedious controversies that ripped the Church apart in later centuries.[4]

That kind of analysis began in the early Middle Ages, and while it is a necessary part of "faith seeking understanding," Stevenson is surely right that some of the later eucharistic controversies over the presence of Christ are tedious. Faith adoring the mystery seems at times to be eclipsed by faith seeking understanding.

Eucharistic Sacrifice: Introduction

The aspect of eucharistic theology to which Bishop Stevenson has given most attention is the Eucharist as sacrifice. The Catholic sacramental theologian, David Power, has described Stevenson's book, *Eucharist and Offering*, in positive terms: "A valiant effort to resolve the problems inherent in the tradition on eucharistic sacrifice by a historical study of texts, principally liturgical, and the application of some contemporary hermeneutical categories."[5] Solid praise from an accomplished sacramental theologian like Power.

Stevenson's concern has been both ecumenical and liturgical. Appropriate attention to liturgical history shows that sacrifice has been a central aspect of the Eucharist from the beginning. Appropriate attention to that aspect necessarily has implications for the unity of the church, since eucharistic sacrifice has been a key point of division and contention between Catholics and Protestants since the Reformation of the sixteenth century, as we have seen throughout this book. Put bluntly but not inaccurately, Catholics approved of the Eucharist as sacrifice and Protestants strongly disapproved. After almost half a millennium of polemic and debate the tide is now turning on this issue in the direction of greater understanding and harmony.

Story, Gift, Response:
The Dimensions of Sacrifice

Stevenson suggests that sacrifice is marked by three criteria: story, gift, response. Story is "the solemn recitation before God of his mighty acts, culminating in the life and work of Christ."[6] As he establishes at great length—using the eucharistic prayers of the entire tradition, East and West as well as within the West after the sixteenth century—the story element varies in length and style from one tradition to another. The "story" is sacrificial because it highlights the liturgical assembly's commitment to "certain activities and spiritual insights." Something valuable and desirable is surrendered in the face of something else having a higher claim. These activities and spiritual insights that flow from the story of God's saving acts in the past commit the assembly to the performance of that story now, and so not to the performance of other stories, alternative narratives of life, with their specific values. Thus, story is sacrificial. As Stevenson puts it, "[S]tory provides the *context* of the Eucharist."[7] The second criterion is "gift": "…the way in which the prayers describe and treat the bread and wine, whether by offering them or by referring to them explicitly or implicitly as gifts."[8] If story provides the sacrificial context of the Eucharist, "[g]ift describes the *material* of the Eucharist."[9] This is probably the sacrificial dimension of the Eucharist with which we are most familiar. We speak of the offertory procession bringing up the "gifts." We speak of the eucharistic elements as "the gifts" also, transformed to transform their recipients. The third criterion of sacrifice is "response": "…what the Church wants the Eucharist to mean and do, as the faithful unite themselves to the sacrifice of Christ."[10] Response can be easily misunderstood. It is not the church as a collection of responsible human beings becoming sacrificial in its own life, so to speak. It is the church, enabled and empowered by the eucharistic gifts, living out of that donation the life of sacrifice. Thus, "Response expresses the action of the Eucharist."[11] It might be thought that Stevenson's three criteria are somewhat too neat to accommodate the complex reality of eucharistic sacrifice. He is himself aware of that as he shows how in the pendulum swinging of the entire Christian tradition, at times "gift" is accentuated, while at other times—the Reformation, for example—"story" as scripture is given emphasis. But Stevenson's methodology for approaching sacrifice has the great merit of submitting that *all* worship is sacrificial. Further, once the "story" and "response" dimensions are understood as sacrificial then the "gift" dimension, the traditionally contested dimension, will look after itself. "If we are Catholic, we can learn to see [sacrifice] in a wider context; if Protestant, we can learn to be less afraid of it."[12] Let us attempt to flesh this out.

Eucharist as Sacrifice

Stevenson sets out a number of issues that have been a barrier not only between the churches on the Eucharist as sacrifice, but in modern society with the concept of sacrifice as such. The first has to do with the basic psychological reaction of many that "sacrifice" belongs to the ancient pagan religions, conjuring up revulsion among modern people. In response to this, Stevenson makes this point: "In a world that knows about suffering in its own way, the metaphor of sacrifice has returned, with a new and vibrant meaning, for our own generation."[13] Second is the notion that eucharistic sacrifice is not biblical:

> This objection is the most fundamental of all, and it is the one most likely to come from the very Protestant side of Christianity, which protests that Christ died once and for all and there is nothing that Christians can do at the Supper other than commemorate that unique and drastic event.[14]

Stevenson points out that the accounts of the Last Supper are charged with "the atmosphere of sacrifice," and the notion is found in the New Testament too, for example, in 1 Peter 2:5: "…and like living stones, let yourselves be built into a spiritual house, to be a holy priesthood, to offer spiritual sacrifices acceptable to God through Jesus Christ." Says Stevenson, "It is hard to imagine the term 'spiritual sacrifices' not including acts of worship, especially the Eucharist itself."[15] To the third objection that sacrifice is a barbaric notion "for which our sophisticated modern world has no room," the bishop indicates that "the aroma of sacrifice persists." He provides examples: from literature William Golding's novel, *Lord of the Flies;* from recent history the term *holocaust,* by definition a sacrificial term, "gained a horrific place in the dictionary of human violence."[16] Sacrifice as such has a firm footing in our modern world. Fourth is the somewhat superficial ecumenical objection, namely, that since we have come such a long way in mutual openness and welcome, it seems a pity to jeopardize that ecumenical progress by focusing on a notion that trails in its wake strife and discord. Stevenson will have none of it. He emphasizes that "[t]he mainstream Churches of the West have rediscovered the Eucharist," and that very rediscovery involves a fresh appreciation of sacrifice. To highlight something of this fresh appreciation of eucharistic sacrifice Stevenson proceeds to see various parts of the Eucharist in the light of sacrifice, so that sacrifice runs throughout the entire celebration and is not confined to the eucharistic gifts alone.

The sixteenth-century reformers desired a strong link between word and sacrament, a link they judged to have been lost in medieval liturgy. They understand the church, the liturgical assembly, to be gathered around the word, to hear that word, to receive that word. May the Liturgy of the Word not be understood in sacrificial terms? Stevenson maintains that it may. This is his "story" dimension of sacrifice at work. The Liturgy of the Word has been described as the "sacrifice of attention."[17] The offering in the Liturgy of the Word is of lips that offer praise to God and of hearts that are receptive to that word. We have to give up our egocentricity, sacrifice it, in order to hear God's word of transforming life. We have to give up, sacrifice a primary focus on ourselves in order genuinely to offer praise to God, the source of life and blessing. Indeed, even the homily may be understood as sacrificial, and Stevenson points to the patristic figure of St. John Chrysostom for support. Chrysostom described the activity of preaching as *thusia,* a Greek word that means "sacrifice." In Stevenson's interpretation, Chrysostom intended by this usage a variety of meanings: the "agony-and-ecstasy" of regular preaching, the process of putting together a fresh homily on an already familiar text, preaching on a difficult subject. Preaching the word is sacrificial because it costs as one tries to communicate something about God for the world.

The prayers of intercession in the Eucharist may also be regarded as sacrificial. "Intercession is a means of identification with the world, not an escape,"[18] and the prayers of intercession are sacrificial because the test of sincere intercession is the degree to which one is committed to doing something about what is being prayed for. "The underlying message is that you cannot pray *for* someone without in some sense committing yourself to doing something about it."[19] Authentic doing is self-sacrificial. It costs.

Then, of course, the eucharistic prayer invites the worshipers to enter into the movement of Christ's unique sacrifice represented in this particular celebration. As they enter into this sacrifice as church, the worshipers are conformed more and more to Christ sacrificed. That conformity bears fruit as they leave the celebration, risen and renewed, to maintain the witness of the church in the world. "The key to the concluding part of the Eucharist is that it is supposed to bring home to the gathered community its own oblation of itself."[20] The eucharistic community, sent into the world to live out the life of self-donation celebrated in the Eucharist and given the grace to do just that, is a sacrificial community.

Bishop Stevenson believes that if both Catholic and Protestant extended their understanding of sacrifice beyond the immediate givens of their own specific ecclesial traditions, the entirety of Christian life and worship would appear as sacrificial, and different traditions would be drawn closer together.[21] If Catholics did not focus almost exclusively on the eucharistic gifts as sacrificial, and Protestants on the proclaimed and preached word as sacrificial, they might enter into greater understanding of the other. This eventually would bear fruit in the closer union of now separated Christians.

Conclusion

Unlike the other theological authors considered in this book, Bishop Kenneth Stevenson is a liturgist by training. His liturgical researches both in the wider Christian tradition as well as in his own Anglican Communion suggest that careful attention to historical detail helps separated Christians to see aspects of the Eucharist that once were considered to be absolutely divisive in a fresh light. This is especially true of the Eucharist as sacrifice, as we have seen.

He believes, however, that Christians need to beware lest the Eucharist "become the *only* act of worship that Christians do together."[22] As Christians lament their present inability to share the Eucharist, they are not thereby prevented from sharing other forms of worship and prayer. Indeed, other forms of worship and prayer, entered into with authenticity at this time, may help prepare the way forward toward unity, and thus in God's time toward eucharistic sharing. Stevenson says:

> Noneucharistic worship, including the liturgy of the hours, should enhance the celebration of the Eucharist. The offering of daily prayer, however structured or formalized, has so much to provide as a way of feeding the prayer life of ordinary Christians. It can serve as a link between Eucharist and the life of service....[23]

Why constantly lament the half-empty glass—the failure to share the Eucharist together in all its fullness—when the half-full glass of noneucharistic worship and prayer remains so untouched?

Notes

1. Kenneth Stevenson, *The First Rites: Worship in the Early Church* (London: Marshall Pickering, 1989).

2. Kenneth Stevenson, *Eucharist and Offering* (New York: Pueblo Publishing Company, 1986); *Accept This Offering: The Eucharist as Sacrifice Today* (London: S.P.C.K., 1989); *Covenant of Grace: A Vision of the Eucharist in the Seventeenth Century* (London: Darton, Longman and Todd, 1994); with the late Henry R. McAdoo, *The Mystery of the Eucharist in the Anglican Tradition* (Norwich: The Canterbury Press, 1995).

3. Kenneth Stevenson, *Nuptial Blessing: A Study of Christian Marriage Rites,* (London: Alcuin Club/S.P.C.K., 1982); *To Join Together: The Rite of Marriage* (New York: Pueblo Publishing Company, 1987).

4. Stevenson, *The First Rites*, 58.

5. David N. Power, *The Eucharistic Mystery: Revitalizing the Tradition* (New York: The Crossroad Publishing Company, 1992), 359.

6. Stevenson, *Eucharist and Offering*, 4.

7. Ibid., 7.

8. Ibid., 5.

9. Ibid., 7.

10. Ibid., 6.

11. Ibid., 7.

12. Ibid., 9.

13. Stevenson, *Accept This Offering*, 2.

14. Ibid.

15. Ibid., 3.

16. Ibid., 3–4.

17. Ibid., 24.

18. Kenneth Stevenson, "'Ye shall pray for...': The Intercession," in Kenneth Stevenson, ed., *Liturgy Reshaped (Essays in Honor of Geoffrey Cuming* (London: S.P.C.K., 1982), 34.

19. Stevenson, *Accept This Offering*, 37–38.

20. Ibid., 83.

21. Stevenson, *Eucharist and Offering*, 232–36.

22. Ibid., 232.

23. Ibid.

Chapter 13
ROWAN D. WILLIAMS

Rowan Douglas Williams, born in Wales in 1950, studied theology at the universities of Cambridge and Oxford in England, receiving his doctorate from the latter with a thesis on the theology of the Russian Orthodox theologian, Vladimir Lossky.[1] After teaching theology at Cambridge, Williams became the Lady Margaret Professor of Divinity at Oxford (in succession to Professor John Macquarrie) in 1986. In 1992 he was ordained bishop of Monmouth, and later became archbishop of Wales. In February 2003, Rowan Douglas Williams was elected archbishop of Canterbury.

There are few Anglican theologians as well versed in Orthodox and Roman Catholic theology, as well as his own tradition, than Rowan Williams. He has written a number of important and influential books, to which reference will be made in this essay. Perhaps the best way to introduce Williams is to begin with some of his remarks in an interview published in 1995, entitled "Time and Transformation: A Conversation with Rowan Williams."[2]

What seems to have woken the bishop as a schoolboy to matters theological was not in fact religious studies but literature. The authors who made the most impression on him were Thomas Hardy, John Donne, George Herbert, Henry Vaughan, and Thomas Traherne. For Williams, "[t]heology is not poetry, exactly, but it's close."[3] In fact, he has published two volumes of his own poetry. As well as the poets, major interests for him have included such diverse figures as the German philosopher Hegel, the Swiss Catholic theologian Hans Urs von Balthasar, and the musician Johann Sebastian Bach. Theology for Williams involves a threefold movement that is celebratory, communicative, and critical.

139

The church is always a bit prone to hang on to the "celebratory" mode—where we concentrate on rehearsing and articulating what's been received—and forget that by itself this becomes self-indulgent. The academy, on the other hand, hangs on to the "critical" mode and can forget why there's a discourse there to be analyzed in the first place. And a lot of attempts at evangelism, and some "theologies of" secular reality…stick with the communicative model…and so drift away from both celebration or contemplation and authentic criticism. Ideally, theology is always a three-way conversation between these elements; each is damaged when it's out of touch with the others.[4]

Williams exemplifies what he commends: He is a man of the church, a priest and bishop celebrating the liturgy; he is a critical theologian of the highest caliber as his many individual studies establish. But he is also a preacher, a man of the communicative word:

Ultimately, a good sermon is one that makes you love God more and trust God more. But in the process of helping you love God more and trust God more, it should make that possible love and trust come alive in relation to particular questions or particular crises that an individual or a group may be facing. There's a lot to be said for it really. I actually *like* preaching—it's a bit unfashionable to say it but I do; it's stretching.[5]

Archbishop Williams has published a volume of some of his sermons and shorter pieces, *A Ray of Darkness*.[6]

What Is a Sacrament?

A sacrament is best understood in terms of what it is *for*; "the activity in which they are caught up, which is making human beings holy."[7] Immediately, this gives direction to the entire sacramental order. It exists as God's initiative to sanctify humankind, to enable humankind to share in the very life of God. In describing the sacraments in this way, Williams explicitly follows St. Thomas Aquinas.[8] He also follows St. Thomas's great contemporary, St. Bonaventure, in describing sacraments as *ars Patris*, the "art of the Father," a way of thinking about the sacraments in harmony with the perspectives of the *Catechism of the Catholic Church*.[9] There too we find the sacraments described in artistic forms, though this time the artist is the Holy Spirit, and the sacraments are God's masterpieces. The first piece, though not of course chronologically, of the Father's art is the Logos himself, Jesus Christ. Then, says Williams, "Derivatively, but really, the Church's sacramental action is the Father's art, not our unaided reflection on human existence, nor even our attempt to render present an absent divine act or a distant promise; they are the drawing of believers into the life of the kingdom of God."[10] The sacraments are God's gracious outreach toward humankind, not our attempt to reach God.

All human beings make signs; it is part of what it means to be human, and this is what Christians call in the broadest sense "sacramental," that is sign-making, activity. "Being human, being bodily and being a user of 'signs' are inseparable...symbolic forms are what we live through as humans."[11] All sign making, and the sign making that is art par excellence, is a sign of the Logos, the expressive Word, the art of the Father. The Word became flesh.

> The life and death of Jesus is a sign of God, showing how a human biography formed by God looks. What leads us to say that Jesus's life is sacramental in a uniquely exhaustive way is that this life not only points to God but is the medium of divine action for judgment and renewal.... The effect of Jesus's life and death is...unprecedentedly comprehensive: by offering and effecting forgiveness, and forming a community around this reality, human relationships and potentialities are set free from the paralyzing and self-intensifying consequences of hostility and aggression to each other and to ourselves, from the lethal symbiosis of violence and guilt.[12]

141

A remarkable passage. Jesus shows what a biography formed by God looks like. He is the unique artistic self-expression of the Father. The effect of this unique art of the Father, Jesus, is fleshed out in the most challenging terms: the offering and effecting of forgiveness, the radical healing of human relationships and potentialities. In short, a new creation, a new creation that reflects the life of the communion of the Trinity.

Eucharist

Archbishop Williams seems to shy away from the sacramental principle that would recognize the presence of God in all things. "It is more that the divine presence is apprehended by seeing in all things their difference, their particularity, their 'not-God-ness'...."[13] He finds the notion that the world is somehow "naturally sacramental" problematic, in his own words "a pot-pourri of Jung, Teilhard de Chardin and a certain kind of anthropology... even if in response to some sense that the world itself is charged with glory."[14] There can be little doubt that in some expressions of sacramental theology this form of the sacramental principle is taken to excess so that we are left with a rather immanentist view of God, leading to a view of sacrament to which the paschal mystery of Jesus Christ has little or nothing to add. In other words, he seems to be saying that if the world is "naturally" sacramental, what does Jesus Christ "add" to this?

This perspective of Williams leads us into deep water and wide of our subject matter in this chapter. However, some beginnings of a response must be made. It seems to me that there is no such thing as a purely "natural" view of nature for a Christian. If we understand the natural world to be free of God's all-pervasive presence until the incarnation takes place, then the incarnation becomes well-nigh unintelligible. If somehow the incarnation of our Lord Jesus Christ is not related to the world as already charged with the grandeur of God's presence, it seems to become a sheer "bolt from the blue." But more can be said. If, as Christians profess in the Nicene Creed, Christ is the One through whom all things are made, and in the prologue to St. John's Gospel the Logos is the One without whom nothing came to be (John 1:3; Col 1:15–20), then all creation has what might be termed this "Christ-dimension." Matter or the natural world is already, if we may say, "impregnate" with the presence of the divine Christ. If this be so, it has implications for the Eucharist. Since the Eucharist is Christ's gracious self-gift, sent by the Father and empowered by the Spirit, the natural world is already in a fundamental sense "eucharistic." Williams himself admits this when he affirms: "All bread and all wine are shadowed with their eucharistic use."[15] Undoubtedly he means looking at all bread and wine through this eucharistic lens. Yes, but the bread and the wine already have this Christ-eucharistic impression in and through the very act of creation. The Incarnate Christ, and his sacrament of self-gift in the Eucharist, is given historically and uniquely in the entire event of Jesus Christ, but the foundations of that eucharistic giving are already laid in the creation of the "natural" world.

When the archbishop moves on to speak of the consequences of the use of material things for the Eucharist, he is most eloquent:

> The eucharist hints at the paradox that material things carry their fullest meaning for human minds and bodies— the meaning of God's grace and of the common life thus formed—when they are the medium of *gift*, not instruments of control or object for accumulation.[16]

Appreciation of the Eucharist as gift empowers and enables the appreciation of the entire material universe as gift. The consequences imply "not dominance, but attention and respect" and a "religious economics."[17] In this way one can see an economic and political theology flowing from the Eucharist.

There is a clear recognition, on Williams's part, of our human condition in the celebration of the Eucharist. Our sinfulness points to our fundamental untrustfulness and our inability, at times, to trust God's faithfulness. "We are shown ourselves initially as those who are unable to trust the faithfulness of God."[18] Thus, at the outset of the celebration we have a penitential rite, and in both the Anglican and the Byzantine liturgies of the Eucharist he notes that there is a return "at significant moments to the rhetoric of penitence and unworthiness, up to the very moment of communion."[19] Once we have received the eucharistic gifts in holy communion, we become bonded or covenanted with God and with each other. This bonding takes place, both vertically and horizontally, because "the material elements of bread and wine are to be made holy by the prayer that associates them with the flesh and blood of Jesus."[20] The transformation of the gifts, effected by God in the eucharistic prayer, is the basis for the bond. The initiative is always God's.

In 1982 Williams wrote *Eucharistic Sacrifice: The Roots of a Metaphor*,[21] a response to an essay on eucharistic sacrifice published by Bishop Richard P. C. Hanson.[22] Hanson's essay was expressive more of evangelical Anglicanism, while Williams's represented Anglo-Catholicism. Williams's concern was to show how a too narrow interpretation of sacrifice can lead away from "a many-layered and suggestive area of symbolism."[23] He negotiates his way carefully through the Christian liturgical tradition, East and West, to argue for

> a retrieval of the idea that the effect of Christ's sacrifice is precisely to make us "liturgical" beings, capable of offering ourselves, our praises and our symbolic gifts to a God who we know will receive us in Christ.[24]

The phrasing is most careful. We are "in Christ" through baptism and sustained in him through Eucharist, because of the entire paschal mystery of Christ, celebrated in the Eucharist. Christ's sacrifice has, therefore, made us "liturgical" beings. Our liturgy, our worship, is always from Christ and in Christ to the Father through the Spirit. In the most profound fashion, then, all that comes to the Father from us, and par excellence the Eucharist, is already "in Christ" and dependent upon the unique sacrifice of Christ on Calvary. The unique and costly self-gift of Christ enables our Eucharist and our whole lives flowing from Eucharist to come before the Father as sacrifice. "We, drawn into communion, into participation with God through the mutual giving of Jesus and his Father, have become part of a fellowship initiated and sustained by gift, and to abide in this fellowship is to learn how we can give, to each other and to God."[25] This trinitarian reading of sacrifice both widens the horizon of that notion, and puts paid to any attempt to think of Christian worship

and life except as "in Christ." There can be, therefore, in this perspective no competition between what Christ has done historically
on the cross and what the church continues to do "in Christ" flowing from that unique and unrepeatable event.

> The glorified Christ, crucified and risen, is eternally
> active towards God the Father on our behalf, drawing us
> into the eternal movement of self-giving love that the
> Son or Word directs towards the source of all, the God
> Jesus calls "Abba."[26]

Eucharistic Devotion

Like his Anglican forebears Mascall, Dix, and Pittenger,
Williams is not opposed to eucharistic devotion. "There is a per-
fectly respectable theology which I accept of devotion to the
eucharistic consecrated elements."[27] But he is opposed, as are
Catholics, to isolating this eucharistic presence of Christ "in some
near-total abstraction from the context of the eucharistic action."
This would make no sense. It is the *action* of the Eucharist that pro-
duces the eucharistic gifts, and any isolation from this living and
originating context is distortion of the eucharistic reality. He draws
a helpful parallel:

> It is parallel to the strangeness of doing Christology as if
> the Incarnation could be isolated from the words and
> work of Christ as a miraculous epiphany of divine power
> in conjoining two alien realities.[28]

The power of the words and works of our Lord is intrinsically
dependent upon the theological reality of the incarnation. The
power of the reserved sacrament is the power of the Eucharist as
action and event, the event of the Mass.

Williams shows something of the complex nature of the feast
Corpus Christi in his book on culture.[29] He points out the intricate
social and moral significance of the Corpus Christi feast and
procession in the Middle Ages. As the sacramental presence of

Christ was carried around the city, it expressed with great power not only the social bonding of people through the Eucharist, by the grace of God, but also how society works through the crisscrossing of frames of meaning:

> What is shown here is not only the meaning of social bondedness in relation to the act of God and the worshipping community, but…the way in which that social meaning works, by a kind of "nesting" of frames of reference within each other: the social body, the Church as Body of Christ, the sacramental presence of Christ's body in the Eucharist; a subtle crossing and recrossing of the boundaries between fields of discourse.[30]

The charity engendered by the complex celebration of Corpus Christi involved the renunciation and transcendence of social rivalries that could at times be violent. Corpus Christi made and makes for an alternative society.

Conclusion

Thus far, Archbishop Rowan Williams has not given his attention to a systematic account of the Eucharist. In this respect he is not unlike David Ford or Graham Ward, the subjects of chapters 11 and 14. Nevertheless, his eucharistic reflections are very close to both Catholics and the Orthodox, while remaining profoundly Anglican. Toward the end of an essay on Eastern Orthodox theology he provides an account of eucharistic ecclesiology:

> The eucharist is thus also the foundation of true, ecclesial *sobornost* ("fellowship"). In it, we come to share fellowship not only with one another, but with the whole company of heaven and the entire cosmos; we do so because we here make contact with a humanity free from the limits of ordinary individuality, a humanity belonging to our history yet not sealed off in the past by death. And in the eucharistic fellowship…human community

becomes the image of the divine: The Church...is the image of the Trinity.[31]

This is surely essential to any genuine Roman Catholic or Anglican theology too. Although in any ecumenical dialogue it will remain important that the details of eucharistic theology be sorted out so that a systematic, comprehensive vision of Eucharist becomes central, without this wider eucharistic vision ultimate perspective is lost. Rowan Williams witnesses to this wider eucharistic perspective that engenders hope for the ecumenical future, and especially for the ecumenical future of Rome and Canterbury.

Notes

1. His essay, "The Via Negativa and the Foundations of Theology: An Introduction to the Thought of V. N. Lossky," appeared in Stephen Sykes and Derek Holmes, eds., *New Studies in Theology* (London: Duckworth, 1980), 95–117.

2. Todd Breyfogle, "Time and Transformation: An Interview with Rowan Williams," *Cross Currents* 45 (1995): 293–311.

3. Ibid., 296.

4. Ibid., 303–4.

5. Ibid., 306.

6. Rowan D. Williams, *A Ray of Darkness* (Boston: Cowley Publications, 1995).

7. Rowan D. Williams, "The Nature of a Sacrament," in John Greenhalgh and Elizabeth Russell, eds., *Signs of Faith, Hope and Love: The Christian Sacraments Today* (London: St. Mary's Bourne Street, 1987), 32. This essay has been reprinted in Rowan D. Williams, *On Christian Theology* (Oxford: Blackwell, 2000), 197–208. Reference here is to the original publication.

8. *Summa Theologiae*, III.60.2c and ad 1.

9. Williams, "The Nature of a Sacrament," 42.

10. Ibid.

11. Ibid., 36–37.

12. Ibid., 39–41.

13. Rowan D. Williams, "Sacraments of the New Society," in David Brown and Ann Loades, eds., *Christ the Sacramental Word* (London: S.P.C.K., 1996), 98. This essay has been reprinted in Williams's *On Christian Theology*, 209–21. Here reference is made to the original essay.

14. Williams, "The Nature of a Sacrament," 36.

15. Ibid., 43.

16. Williams, "Sacraments of the New Society," 98.

17. Ibid., 99.

18. Ibid., 95.

19. Ibid.

20. Ibid.

21. Rowan D. Williams, *Eucharistic Sacrifice: The Roots of a Metaphor* (Bramcote, Notts.: Grove Books, 1982).

22. Richard P. C. Hanson, *Eucharistic Offering in the Early Church* (Bramcote, Notts.: Grove Books, 1979).

23. Williams, *Eucharistic Sacrifice*, 32.

24. Ibid., 27.

25. Ibid., 29.

26. Rowan D. Williams, "Foreword," to Henry R. McAdoo and Kenneth Stevenson, *The Mystery of the Eucharist in the Anglican Tradition* (Norwich: Canterbury Press, 1995), x.

27. Williams, "The Nature of a Sacrament," 42.

28. Ibid., 42–43.

29. Rowan D. Williams, *Lost Icons: Reflections on Cultural Bereavement* (Edinburgh: T. & T. Clark, 2000), 54–56.

30. Ibid., 55.

31. Rowan D. Williams, "Eastern Orthodox Theology," in David F. Ford, ed., *The Modern Theologians*, 2nd ed. (Oxford: Blackwell, 1997), 509.

Chapter 14

GRAHAM WARD AND CATHERINE PICKSTOCK

Graham Ward, professor of contextual theology and ethics at the University of Manchester, England, and a priest of the Church of England, and Catherine Pickstock of Emmanuel College, the University of Cambridge, are both members of what has come to be known as the "radical orthodoxy" movement. This is a theological movement mainly associated with the University of Cambridge, England, intent on speaking and writing against secular modernity and its denial of the transcendent. Along with John Milbank, Ward and Pickstock are the leading lights behind this Cambridge movement, the origins probably lying in John Milbank's book, *Theology and Social Theory.*[1] The central thesis of the book is that many supposedly secular disciplines, for example, sociology, political science, literary theory, and philosophy, operate with implicit religious and theological assumptions. Milbank (and now his colleagues in the radically orthodox movement) wishes to demonstrate "the vicious theologies" of these supposedly secular disciplines and replace them with "virtuous theologies" that draw upon pre-Reformation traditions, especially biblical and patristic. As a movement "radical orthodoxy" is not well known outside academic circles, and so it will be helpful to provide some basic information about it and its objectives.

A useful introduction to radical orthodoxy is afforded in an interview conducted by Rachel Kohn, a British journalist, with John Milbank and Catherine Pickstock at Emmanuel College, Cambridge, and broadcast on Sunday, November 7, 1999.[2] In response to "What's radical about radical orthodoxy?" John Milbank had this to say:

All orthodoxies are radical in the sense that they are attempts to return to the roots, and living roots are never things that are fixed once and for all, they are always regenerating, so that I think that any radical movement has something to do with reasserting the origins, reasserting what's different about a tradition.

In returning to roots and reasserting origins, Milbank maintains that this is no nostalgic return to the past: "We don't think that [the past] was ever perfect." In the interview Pickstock is even more specific than Milbank.

There's a tendency because we call ourselves orthodox at all, and because we're drawing on the tradition of Plato, Augustine, Aquinas particularly, we're seen as somehow wishing to turn back the clock, and recoup identically the Middle Ages, and that's absolutely not what we're doing....We're not in that kind of nostalgic rejection, but we're trying to challenge everything by drawing upon all these other resources, but we're not trying to turn backwards against the forward flow of time.

Biblical, patristic, and medieval traditions become the resources for challenging the secularist assumptions of modernity. These past periods of Christian history are not viewed by the radically orthodox as some kind of golden age that needs to be reestablished. However, it is from these traditions cumulatively that the radically orthodox can build up their positions. The radically orthodox are opposed to any dualist tendencies that might in principle suggest a fundamental dualism between the divine and the created order, so that the latter may be had without the former. Such fragmentary tendencies are characteristic of the Reformation, the Enlightenment, and consequent modernity.

For Pickstock the center of the Christian tradition is worship:

It's only really in the act of worship that one is fully oneself. But at the same time, more than oneself, because in that, you can't sort of offer something to God without in some sense becoming one with God.

From the point of view of liturgical theology Pickstock's comment is most attractive, even as it seems at first sight a very tall claim to make. Her presuppositions are in fact articulated in her important book, *After Writing: The Liturgical Consummation of Philosophy.*[3] Though she has not in this quotation in the interview actually mentioned the Eucharist, what she says is an accurate description of the nature and purpose of the Eucharist, that is to say, that we are most fully ourselves in Eucharist, because, in and through God's gracious gift of self, we are participating in the very life of the Divine Communion. Our fullest self is participant in divinity. In fact, anything may be rightly understood only in relation to God, who is the fullness of being. Awareness of participation in the divine life needs to pervade everything.

> The central theological framework of radical orthodoxy is "participation" as developed by Plato and reworked by Christianity, because any alternative configuration perforce reserves a territory independent of God....The latter can lead only to nihilism....Every discipline must be framed by a theological perspective; otherwise, these disciplines will define a zone apart from God, grounded literally in nothing.[4]

One implication, therefore, of radical orthodoxy is that there is no such thing as "the secular," if one means by the secular that which is cut off from any reference to the divine. Milbank puts it well in the interview: "The secular itself is the creation of a particular kind of theology, a kind of theology that no longer was grounded in participation, and instead gave finitude a kind of strange autonomy...." Secularism, which pits religious faith against reason and science and, moreover, insists upon the hegemony of science, is a one-dimensional view of the universe utterly opposed by radical orthodoxy. For the radically orthodox there is no such thing as the secular.

Graham Ward and the Eucharist

Two essays by Graham Ward have implications for the Eucharist, though neither of them could immediately be construed as eucharistic theology. The first essay is "Transcorporeality: The Ontological Scandal"[5] (hereafter "Transcorporeality") and "Bodies: The Displaced Body of Jesus Christ"[6] (hereafter "Bodies").

Influenced by the theology of Karl Barth, Ward maintains:

> Theology reads Scripture, the traditions of the Church and the world in the light of the glory of the Risen Christ in the space opened between that resurrection [and ascension] and our own.[7]

The church for him is what we might call the "expanded" Jesus Christ, occupying time and space in the time and space opened up by his resurrection and ascension. This will continue to grow until the parousia, when God finalizes reality as he will have it be. This is the narrative or story recounted in Holy Scripture, and the church is that privileged body whose witness is the living out of the Christ-story in succeeding generations. Ward is fond of textual metaphors, and so he writes:

> The practices of Christian living parse the divine grammar: in our words and our worlding we are adverbial in the sense Eckhart gives that part of speech when he prays: "may the Father, the Verbum (the Word), and the Holy Spirit help us to remain adverbs of this Verbum (Word)."[8]

Christian living becomes in-scription in the Word, words in the Word, adverbs of the Word. The implication seems clear: Anyone "reading" the text of our Christian lives is reading the Word in the words that we are.

Close to the beginning of "Transcorporeality" Ward writes:

> I want to talk about the racked and viral-ridden bodies of the beautiful, the power-hungry and disenfranchised

bodies of the polis, the torn and bleeding body of the Church, the poisoned and raped body of the world and the abused body of Jesus Christ.[9]

To say the least, this is a very challenging sentence. Disease and illness, violence both political and ecological, are brought into connection with the "abused body of Jesus Christ." Right away the suggestion is being made that any dualisms are unacceptable, and we are implicitly invited to ask, "Why?" The answer:

> Christian theology offers a profound thinking about the nature of bodies through the relationship it weaves between creation, incarnation, ecclesiology and eucharist.[10]

There is a continuum, enabled and empowered by God, between creation, Christ, the church, and the Eucharist. The profundity of thinking emerges from "the depths of an ontological scandal," the scandal of the word is in the sentence "Take, eat, this *is* my body."[11] The scandal of the word *is* is expressed in the renaming of a piece of bread as the body of Jesus Christ. The ontological scandal is demonstrated by Ward when he uses the parallel of holding up a piece of cheese and saying, "Here is the moon." This is scandalously unreasonable, given the publicly accepted sense of what is to be taken as "reasonable."

In the ordinary, taken-for-granted philosophy of the modern world, identifying a piece of bread, held up, as the body of Jesus Christ is an act of madness. It is an act of madness because "[n]aming relies upon social consensus and memory of past, confirming acts of identification."[12] In other words, we do not simply see or perceive things so much as we are socialized to name things as these particular things.

> The world asserts its own reality. Behind such a view lies an atomism: ultimate reality is found in the independence of each atom asserting its own self-enclosed being.[13]

Faced, then, with a piece of bread named as the body of Jesus Christ within this commonsensical approach to reality only three responses are possible: doubting what is observed ("It does not look like the body of Jesus Christ"); mistaken identification as a result of mental challenges ("There is something wrong with you if you think this bread is the body of Jesus Christ"); or, it is a "miracle" in the very precise Enlightenment sense that prevails in most textbooks on the philosophy of religion, that is to say, an event that appears unexplainable by the laws of nature, as construed socially, and so is held to be supernatural in origin or an act of God. In other words, "miracle" interrupts what we know to be the normative rules and laws of reality. The most "reasonable" response in our modern culture, Ward maintains, would be the second one. It is an act of madness to identify a piece of bread with the body of Jesus Christ.

What, however, if we do not begin with this ordinary, taken-for-granted philosophy of the modern world? What would be the reception of the identification of a piece of bread with the body of Jesus Christ if we refused to privilege this commonsensical philosophy and, instead, privileged the Christian neo-Platonism of the fourth century father of the church, Gregory of Nyssa? Without going into the rich details of Gregory's writings, we may summarize his viewpoint in this way:

> Nature cannot be natural without the spiritual informing
> it at every point....Materiality is a manifestation of
> divine *energeia*, a mode of trinitarian *dunamis*.[14]

Energeia means "operation, working," and *dunamis* "power." So, for Gregory, nature or matter is never absent of the divine. God is always at work in nature. There is no such thing as nature or matter without God's operation or power. There is no absolute dualism. This perspective stands in clear contrast with the modern, commonsensical, empirical perspective that identifies the real with what may be seen and touched, with what may be accessed through one's senses. The real is only real for Gregory (and by implication for Christians) when it is seen as suffused with the divine, with the spiritual. There can be no interruption of the divine into reality, because that would imply that reality existed separately from the divine. Or, as Ward puts it himself:

Corporeality has to be read spiritually.... Creation, as the manifestation of God through his Word, is a text which it is the vocation of human being, made in the image of that God, to be read and understood.[15]

If God is genuinely manifesting himself through nature, through matter, so that it is inconceivable apart from God, then wonder-full things will happen, miracles will occur, including the miracle of bread and wine becoming the body and blood of Jesus Christ.

The ontological scandal here concerns God's uncreated power to bring being from nothing, bring flesh from bread. The scandal is the giftedness of being itself—that something should be rather than not be—which the transformative word of God announces.[16]

God's calling creation into being implies that God's being is the very being of creation, but not in a pantheistic direction. God is prior, and it is God's being in which creation participates. There is literally no such thing as an autonomous, entirely independent object or entity apart from the reality of God.

There is only one radical critique of modernity—the critique that denies the existence of the secular, that immanent self-ordering of the world which ultimately had no need for God.[17]

This is, in fact, the critique of the radically orthodox. Nothing is ever understood unless it is understood in relation to God. Apart from God, there "is" only nihilism!

Ward has a nice turn of phrase for this theocentrism, this Christocentrism. Since all of creation has come from the Word of God (John 1:3, "All things came into being through him, and without him not one thing came into being"), "all creation bears the watermark of Christ."[18] A dictionary definition of *watermark* is "a translucent design impressed on paper during manufacture and visible when the finished paper is held to the light." When creation is held up to the light, as it were, we can see the mark of Jesus Christ within it. Creation is in, through, and for Christ. The christocentric insight may be pushed further. Within this horizon of God-energized matter, there is a eucharistic impulse to reality as such. Eucharist, from its Greek root *eucharistein*, means "to give thanks." All creation shares this eucharistic impulse because there is no necessity for it to exist, "the giftedness of creation out of nothing."[19] All creation implicitly "thanks" God for the free gift of its existence. This is what Ward is getting at when he says, "The world is a eucharistic offering: it continues to exist as a giving of thanks for its very givenness."[20] To be is to be eucharistic. The celebration of the Eucharist brings this impulse to explicit and rational awareness. As Ward has it:

> All things feed each other—that is the nature of their participation in God. Christ as the bread of life feeds our rational beings that we might continue to discern and desire God in all things.[21]

All creation is an expansive network of participation in the divine, making all existence essentially relational, and especially human existence: "We belong to Jesus and Jesus to others through partaking of his given body. We exist in and through relation."[22]

Reality, understood relationally and christocentrically and eucharistically, is being transformed as it moves eschatologically toward the parousia. This final consummation of all reality is anticipated in the Eucharist, and, under grace, is furthered in the Eucharist. Christ leading to church, church made by Eucharist, anticipates and signals the growth of Christ's presence until the End. This is how Ward expresses it:

> The eucharistic fracture, repeating differently the crucifixion, disseminates the body—of Christ and the Church as the body of Christ. The dissemination sets each body free to follow…within the plenitude of the Word which passes by and passes on. What initiates the following after is the awareness of our being involved, of our having been drawn into the ongoing divine activity. Our

being involved is a tasting of that which we know we long for; we drink of eternal life in that participation.[23]

Receiving the Christ in holy communion enables the deep and radical following of Christ. The power to follow comes from that reception. It is the power of grace, and not merely human effort. However, and this is what is accentuated in the last part of the citation, our finding-following Christ is first Christ's finding-following us. We are *drawn into* the divine activity through the Eucharist. "The structure of Christian desire is, significantly, twofold—not only my desire, but God's desire for me."[24]

Catherine Pickstock and the Eucharist

Perhaps we may say for Catherine Pickstock that there are two fundamental visions of life and reality. The first vision is that in which the modern, atomized subject moves through the course of a life, characteristically marked by dualisms: private-public, sacred-secular, everyday work-weekend leisure, and so forth. At its best, liturgy becomes in this vision a moment of relief or retreat from the rest of life. The second vision sees life and all reality from liturgy, in relation to liturgy, in such a way that dualisms disappear. It is this second vision, in line with radical orthodoxy as described earlier, that is Catherine Pickstock's.

This second vision of seeing liturgy at the heart of reality is approaching the liturgy as *theologia prima*, primary theology. This is not the actual language Pickstock uses, but this is her understanding: "It is in the enactment of liturgical offering that we enter the site of maximum mediation of theological reflection in the practical realm."[25] Describing liturgy in a most general fashion, Pickstock equally describes the Eucharist: "The everyday reaches perpetually beyond itself in worship."[26] Joy and sorrow mark the human every day, but in worship the human reaches beyond them. In the celebration of the Eucharist, individual joys are seen as "specific manifestations of a continuous collective celebration," while personal sorrows are viewed "in the context of cosmic patterns which include such tragic eventualities."[27] Redemption and transfiguration are made possible and rendered conscious and aware in the liturgy. God, the gracious Beyond, reaches down to us in liturgy, centered in Eucharist, and from this divine *telos* "liturgy imagines a world perhaps of angels, for example, that is seen as more real than the given, and which holds out the telos to which the given aspires, and which alone defines what the 'given' is."[28] Every liturgical celebration becomes a moment of real openness to the Divine Transcendence, even as God enables and invites transformation through that liturgical moment. In summary, then:

> It is assumed within the logic of Christian liturgy, that if one goes to the altar, which prefigures the altar set in the middle of the heavenly Jerusalem, then one does so *as oneself*, and in fact *only becomes oneself* in doing so at all; and indeed, in doing this, one really does go up to the heavenly Jerusalem.[29]

Pickstock wishes to show that the whole identity of the church is eucharistic: "This means that the Church is only the Body of Christ insofar as it receives the Body of Christ, that is to say, receives *itself* from the eucharist."[30] She has a knack of putting this central insight that the Eucharist makes the church in many complementary and fine ways, for example: "...the continuing coming-to-be of the Church as Christ's body [is] through an ingesting of this same body which is at once a real and a symbolic consuming."[31] Another beautiful example: "Supremely, the church as 'Body of Christ' was ceaselessly recreated through receiving the gift of the eucharistic Body of Christ."[32] This is theology with which any Catholic might easily resonate.

This polysemic meaning of "Body of Christ" is only possible if there is a basic realism to the eucharistic gifts themselves. There is an equivalence between the eucharistic words of Jesus and the later doctrine of transubstantiation. Pickstock follows Aquinas here.

> When Aquinas finds that transubstantiation has been effected in such a way that the accidents of bread and wine nonetheless remain, one could say that he is strictly adhering to the peculiar linguistic pragmatics of this New Testament usage.[33]

She does not spend much time on the issue of eucharistic sacrifice as such. Her interest is always the bigger picture. Sacrifice for Pickstock is not discrete and atomized eucharistic belief, but expresses the entirety of the divine movement. As the eucharistic elements are offered to God and, in turn, are divinized by God, becoming the sacrament of God-in-Christ's unique self gift on the cross, so there is a holism to sacrifice: "The *whole* of this sacrifice, God Himself, is eaten by every single individual without any exclusion and distinction."[34] Sacrifice belongs in the trinitarian life, as much as it is expressed in the Mass.

Pickstock, albeit as an Anglican, is not an unqualified supporter of the liturgical reforms consequent upon Vatican II, at least those in respect of the Eucharist. For her, "the revisions were simply *not radical enough.*"[35] She accepts the criticisms of the liturgy that it was growing in an overly individualistic direction, and was too often seen as a spectacle to behold. However, the notion that the contemporary reforms required the elimination of "the many uneconomic repetitions and recommencements" was seriously mistaken. Rather than being seen as so many unnecessary accretions to an original, pure liturgy, Pickstock interprets these repetitions and recommencements as liturgical stammering before God. The drafters of the liturgical reform, especially of the Eucharist, flattened out "the liturgical stammer and constant re-beginning" that our creaturely posture before God requires.[36] The old Mass, so to speak, was such that it was quite unclear "what is our own 'initiative' and what is the mediation of the divine by human action."[37] While I find myself in sympathy with her point of view, the fact of the matter is that Catholics have a new rite of the Mass. There can be no going back, but there can be the retrieval, the long and hard retrieval of what was lost in liturgical reform. This is the task of theology, catechesis, and homiletics, and it is ongoing, never ending.

Conclusion

Neither Graham Ward nor Catherine Pickstock provides a packaged sacramental theology of the Eucharist. It is not their interest, at least at this time, to sketch all those theological elements that would need some comment such as, for example, the Eucharist as sacrifice, the eucharistic presence of Christ, though Pickstock more than Ward has much to say here. Ward, and in some degree Pickstock, is more keen to develop and suggest the cosmic backdrop to eucharistic theology construed more narrowly.

Ward and Pickstock want us to feel, quite literally feel and touch a world that in the words of the poet Gerard Manley Hopkins, SJ, is "charged with the grandeur of God." They want to move us away from a view of physical reality that deems it autonomous, brute, inert matter. It can never be that from a Christian perspective. Rather, as charged with God's grandeur the universe is incipiently eucharistic, thanking God for being, and in and after Jesus the Lord it is propelled toward becoming explicitly eucharistic, as it moves from Christ's resurrection to ours. These thoughts and reflections are not novel with Graham Ward and Catherine Pickstock. A careful sifting of the church's tradition would throw them up generation after generation. A careful sifting of Graham Ward's work will show for him—and indeed for the radically orthodox theologians generally —an exciting reacquaintance with the Christian tradition. Gregory of Nyssa is featured alongside Jacques Derrida, the contemporary French philosopher, Meister Eckhart, OP, alongside the late French theorist, Michel de Certeau. The capacity of the Christian tradition to speak afresh is underlined by this juxtaposition of old and new. Let us draw to a close by citing Ward citing the words of St. Symeon the New Theologian, as summing up Ward's own meaning:

> I move my hand, and my hand is the whole of Christ
> since, do not forget it, God is indivisible in his divinity...
> all our members individually will become members of
> Christ and Christ our members.[38]

It is, if you like, the eucharistic big picture that we receive from Ward and Pickstock and that we need to recall if our appreciation of the eucharistic little picture is to continue to grow for us.

Notes

1. John Milbank, *Theology and Social Theory* (Oxford: Blackwell, 1990).

2. The interview was aired on the radio program, "The Spirit of Things," and was entitled "Rejecting Modernity: Radical Orthodoxy," the title we shall refer to in this essay. The full text may be found at www.abc.net.au/rn/relig/spirit/stories/s65244.htm. The text is not paginated numerically, making it impossible to refer to actual pages. Any unreferenced quotation from the radically orthodox authors is from this interview.

3. Catherine Pickstock, *After Writing: The Liturgical Consummation of Philosophy* (Oxford: Blackwell, 1997).

4. John Milbank, Catherine Pickstock, and Graham Ward, eds., *Radical Orthodoxy* (London and New York: Routledge, 1999), 3. See also R. R. Reno, "The Radical Orthodoxy Project," *First Things* (February 2000): 39.

5. Graham Ward, "Transcorporeality: The Ontological Scandal," *Bulletin of the John Rylands Library* 80 (1998): 235–52.

6. In Milbank, Pickstock, and Ward, eds., *Radical Orthodoxy*, 163–81.

7. Ward, "Bodies," 163.

8. Ibid., 175.

9. Ward, "Transcorporeality," 235.

10. Ibid., 236.

11. Ibid.

12. Ibid., 239.

13. Ibid., 241.

14. Ibid., 243.

15. Ibid., 244.

16. Ibid.

17. Ibid., 250.

18. Ward, "Bodies," 165.

19. Ibid., 173.

20. Ward, "Transcorporeality," 246.

21. Ibid.

22. Ward, "Bodies," 169.

23. Ibid., 171.

24. Ibid., 172.

25. Catherine Pickstock, "Medieval Liturgy and Modern Reform," *Antiphon: A Journal for Liturgical Renewal* 6 (2001): 19.

26. Catherine Pickstock, "Liturgy, Art and Politics," *Modern Theology* 16 (2000): 160.

27. Ibid., 161.

28. Ibid., 162.

29. Ibid., 165.

30. Ibid., 174.

31. Catherine Pickstock, "Thomas Aquinas and the Eucharist," *Modern Theology* 15 (1999): 164.

32. Pickstock, "Medieval Liturgy and Modern Reform," 20.

33. John Milbank and Catherine Pickstock, *Truth in Aquinas* (London and New York: Routledge, 2001), 99.

34. Pickstock, "Liturgy, Art and Politics," 175.

35. Pickstock, "Medieval Liturgy and Modern Reform," 20.

36. Ibid., 24.

37. "The Meaning of the Mass: An Interview with Catherine Pickstock," *The Latin Mass* 7 (1998): 45.

38. Ward, "Transcorporeality," 248.

Chapter 15

SUMMARY AND PROSPECT

Only bigots or pessimists could dismiss the real and welcome change in
relations between the Anglican and Roman Catholic Churches, but
even optimists might miss the fundamental character of this change.
(Mary Cecily Boulding, OP)[1]

These words of one who was central to the deliberations and
workings of ARCIC II shape the direction of this final chapter.
There has been real and welcome change between the Anglican
and the Roman Catholic churches. Yet, while the fundamental
character of this change might pass unnoticed by ecumenical
optimists, at the same time it cannot be doubted that ecumenism,
both in the minds of theologians and of many Christian laity, has
fallen on hard times. For example, the late Jean Tillard reported
that not long after the publication of Pope John Paul II's *Ut unum*
sint, theologians professionally engaged in ecumenism thought it
a lost cause.[2] If one feels the pain of Christian disunity, one understands the great frustration of ecumenists and ecumenically
minded Christians.

Before the Mississauga meeting actually took place, there
was hope that that it would be a stimulus toward greater ecumenical commitment between Anglicans and Catholics, as in the
hopeful words of Anglican ecumenist, Mary Tanner: "This might
just provide a kick-start and revive the sort of enthusiasm of the
heady days that followed Vatican II. It would demonstrate that we
have progressed in thirty-two years and would show our determination to go on together."[3] Tanner's hopes have not been disap-
pointed.

The Mississauga Meeting, 2000

At Mississauga near Toronto, from May 14 to 20, 2000, Anglican and Catholic bishops from thirteen countries, led by Archbishop George Carey of Canterbury and Cardinal Edward Cassidy of the Pontifical Council for Christian Unity, met to consult about how ecumenical relations between Canterbury and Rome should now progress. After almost forty years of ecumenical dialogue, both internationally and nationally, it was time to take stock, recognize the good things that have happened, acknowledge the difficulties, and develop a sense of how to move on.

Among the many good things that have taken place are: improvement in local ecumenical relations; clergy at all levels and laity getting to know each other better; the national dialogues, for example, the Anglican-Roman Catholic Dialogues in the United States (ARC-USA) and the international dialogues of the Anglican-Roman Catholic International Commission (ARCIC). The difficulties are obvious: the ordination of women to the presbyterate and episcopate; the question of Anglican orders, condemned by Pope Leo XIII in his *Apostolicae curae* of 1896; the exercise of authority, including the Petrine ministry; some moral and ethical issues. If the tardiness of Rome in responding to the *Final Report* of ARCIC-I suggested to some that union with Canterbury was of secondary importance to Rome, the ways in which the Anglican Communion was dealing with the burning issues of the ordination of women to the presbyterate and the episcopate, without seeming to take adequate account of ecumenical consequences, had the same effect on some Roman Catholics. If we are not to concede to what Tillard calls "the solution of despair," we have an obligation to proceed in hope.

However, although one might reasonably argue that the pace of dialogue between Canterbury and Rome has slowed in recent years, the Toronto meeting augurs well for the future. It produced two statements: *Communion in Mission* and the *Action Plan.* *Communion in Mission* is composed of fourteen points. In the first of these we read: "Our meeting was grounded in prayer and marked by a profound atmosphere of friendship and spiritual communion." The role of prayer is sometimes underrated in the "work" that needs to take place. Prayer is work in the sense that it takes time and effort and a disciplined structure. Otherwise it simply will not happen. Archbishop Alexander J. Brunett of Seattle, Catholic cochair of ARCIC, and Bishop Frank Griswold of the Episcopal Church both attested that two hours a day were spent in prayer during the Toronto meeting.[4] Point four of the statement included a focus on worship. "We realized afresh both the degree of spiritual communion we already share in the richness of our common liturgical inheritance, but also the pain of our inability to share fully in the Eucharist."

The common liturgical inheritance between Canterbury and Rome is very rich indeed. It includes the sacraments of the church, for example. There is also the Liturgy of the Hours, especially morning and evening prayer. It was especially the Anglican celebration of Evensong that captivated the great Catholic ecumenical theologian, Cardinal Yves M. J. Congar, during his stay in England in the early 1950s. Devotion to Mary, mother of God, is yet another central tradition shared by Rome and Canterbury. One could continue to mount examples. This book, for example, *Canterbury Cousins*, has been an attempt to plot something of this rich, shared liturgical and sacramental treasury in the Eucharist. Anglicans and Catholics are on the same eucharistic page, even if some of the details on that page are yet to be received and shared by all. Point six of the statement is quite emphatic about the degree of communion already in place: "We have come to a clear sense that we have moved much closer to the goal of full, visible communion than we had at first dared to believe." This is a wonderful statement, especially when one realizes that it is being made in full awareness of the difficulties between the two communions noted above.

A real breakthrough has taken place in the recommendation of *Communion in Mission* for a "Joint Unity Commission," which would report to both Rome and Canterbury, as it were. It occurs in paragraph 12 of the document. This proposed commission would have a host of ecumenical responsibilities. Perhaps the most important of these is its implementation of "reception in the churches of the theological consensus already achieved through nearly four decades of dialogue."[5] This joint commission is now known as the International Anglican Roman Catholic Commission for Unity and

Mission, and by the acronym IARCCUM. If the commission can find ways of enabling the churches to receive this theological consensus, much will have been achieved. Speaking only for Catholics, too many have no informed awareness of doctrines and positions *shared* with Anglicans. Reception must, therefore, be seen as of the greatest priority.

From our perspective in this book, it is paragraph 13 that is most explicitly eucharistic:

> Our vision of full and visible unity is of a eucharistic communion of churches: confessing the one faith and demonstrating by their harmonious diversity the richness of faith.... This eucharistic communion on earth is a participation in the larger communion which includes the saints and martyrs, and all those who have fallen asleep in Christ through the ages.

The vision of unity is of a "eucharistic communion," and the achievement of such communion is absolutely dependent upon a common Eucharist. That is the goal to which both Rome and Canterbury are moving.

The Eucharistic Ellipse

The theologians considered in this book represent some of the best modern and contemporary theological minds in the Anglican Communion. While they are not easily categorized, it may be helpful to think of their contribution in the following way. Gore, Spens, Quick, Mascall, Dix, Mackinnon, and Pittenger, and in a different way Hanson, deal substantially with the eucharistic issues that have been divisive since the Reformation, and most especially the doctrines of eucharistic presence and sacrifice, as well as the practices of eucharistic reservation and devotion that receive various degrees of support, as we have seen. Let us call these the microeucharistic issues, the "small picture" of doctrinal concerns that constitute the reality of the Eucharist. Williams and Stevenson continue this tradition, but not, so it seems to me, with the holistic vision and detail that their named theological forebears represent. Ford, Ward, and Pickstock, on the other hand, while acknowledging the microeucharistic issues, are more interested in treating the macroeucharistic issues, the bigger picture of concerns that impinge upon our appreciation of the Eucharist: praise and poetry, the eucharistic self, the ontology of creation and the Eucharist, the relation of liturgy to life. Both are necessary for any finally adequate appreciation. Both are present in the Windsor Statement, but with the emphasis probably on the microeucharistic questions. The macro and micro themes are like the two focuses of an ellipse. Take out one focus and the ellipse collapses. If the ellipse of the Eucharist is to be the graced, creative basis for the eucharistic communion of Canterbury and Rome, both focuses need attention, as each will give determination and shape to the other.

In his Père Marquette Lecture for the year 2000, the veteran ecumenical and liturgical theologian, Geoffrey Wainwright, surveyed with broad-brush strokes as well as attention to detail matters ecumenical at the start of the new millennium.[6] Among many points he makes were the following: that while there is undeniably a justified pluralism of theological interpretation, care must be taken so that it does not "sink into dogmatic indifferentism."[7] In respect of the Eucharist between Catholics and Anglicans, there seems little danger of dogmatic indifferentism. Care and attention have been and are being paid to the nexus of eucharistic meanings treasured and maintained in both traditions. The subjects of this book witness to that. Wainwright also asks the question, "Are doctrinal matters between Catholics and Protestants now settled?" and provides the appropriate answer, "More than they were."[8] Christians experience joy that the Holy Spirit has moved them closer together—"more than they were"—and sensitivity and care not to diminish with indifferentism the doctrinal differences that remain.

Conclusion

Mary Cecily Boulding, OP, evaluating Anglican-Catholic ecumenical progress since Vatican II, concludes:

The last forty years could be described as a progress from euphoria, through acute depression to an equilibrium characterized by hard grind, illustrating perhaps the recognized stages of growth to maturity—optimism, pessimism, realism.[9]

This description holds true primarily of church leaders and of people professionally involved in ecumenism. That growth, from optimism through pessimism to realism, must now invite and encourage the hard grind at the local level, and for the "ordinary people in the pews."

At the end of the first chapter, "Introducing Canterbury and Rome," are found the following words: "My hope and prayer is that those who look to Canterbury as the center of their Christian communion, and celebrate and reflect upon the Eucharist in the tradition of Canterbury will be seen by Catholics as cousins, and cousins to whom in God's grace we are drawing closer." It is for the reader to judge whether this ecumenical hope has been borne out by the presentation of this sample of Anglican theologians and perspectives concerning the Eucharist. If *Canterbury Cousins* leads to a greater concern among his fellow Catholics for ecumenism, and to the books and papers of the theologians considered, the author will be well pleased.

Notes

1. Mary C. Boulding, "Anglican-Roman Catholic Relations Since Vatican II," *The Downside Review* 121 (2003): 26.

2. Jean Tillard, "Roman Catholics and Anglicans: Is There a Future for Ecumenism?" *One in Christ* 32 (1996): 106.

3. Mary Tanner, "Anglican-Roman Catholic Relations from Malta to Toronto," *One in Christ* 36 (2000): 122.

4. John Borelli, "Renewal for Anglican-Roman Catholic Relations," *America* (August 26–September 2, 2000): 15.

5. Ibid., 14.

6. Geoffrey Wainwright, *Is the Reformation Over? Catholics and Protestants at the Turn of the New Millennia* (Milwaukee, WI: Marquette University Press, 2000).

7. Ibid., 26.

8. Ibid., 27.

9. Boulding, "Anglican-Roman Catholic Relations Since Vatican II," 26.

INDEX OF NAMES